SELF REMEMBERING

THE PATH TO NON-JUDGMENTAL LOVE

Poetry Books by Red Hawk

Journey of the Medicine Man (August House, 1983)
The Sioux Dog Dance (Cleveland State University, 1991)
The Way of Power (Hohm Press, 1996)
The Art of Dying (Hohm Press, 1999)
Wreckage with a Beating Heart (Hohm Press, 2005)
Raven's Paradise, winner: Bright Hill Press Poetry Prize (2010)
The Indian Killer (Anjaneya Press, 2013), signed and numbered,
limited edition

Non-fiction Book by Red Hawk

Self Observation: The Awakening of Conscience: An Owner's Manual
(Hohm Press, 2009)

SELF REMEMBERING

THE PATH TO NON-JUDGMENTAL LOVE

A Practitioner's Manual

RED HAWK

Hohm Press
Chino Valley, Arizona

Cover Design: Adi Zuccarello

Interior Design and Layout: Becky Fulker, Kubera Book Design, Prescott, AZ

Library of Congress Cataloging-in-Publication Data

Red Hawk.
  Self remembering : the path to non-judgmental love : a practitioner's manual / Red Hawk.
     pages cm
  Includes bibliographical references and index.
  ISBN 978-1-935387-92-3 (trade pbk. : alk. paper)
  1. Uspenskii, P. D. (Petr Dem'ianovich), 1878-1947--Teachings. 2. Fourth Way (Occultism) 3. Self-consciousness (Awareness) 4. Awareness. 5. Memory. 6. Love--Miscellanea. 7. Spiritual life. I. Title.
  BP605.G9R43 2015
  158.1--dc23
                    2014047872

Hohm Press
P.O. Box 4410
Chino Valley, AZ 86323
800-381-2700
http://www.hohmpress.com

This book was printed in the U.S.A. on recycled, acid-free paper using soy ink.

Dedication

This book is in the Grateful service of Mister Lee,
Who dwells in the Sacred Heart of Mercy
with His Father, Yogi Ramsuratkumar:

All praise is Yours;
we are in Your hands, in Your eyes,
and beg to be surrendered in Your Sacred Heart;

everything is Yours.
Where can we go where You are not?
Guide us and provide that

which serves You.
Please remove all obstacles and
by Your Grace and Mercy
Surrender us in Non-Judgmental Love.

There are servants of God
whom God favors with blessings
for the service of others
and whom God keeps supplied
as long as they are generous
with what they have.
For if they refuse or withhold,
God takes those favors away from them
and transfers them to others.

—*Living and Dying with Grace:*
Counsels of Hadrat Ali. Translated by
Thomas Cleary, 105.

❧

I am deeply indebted for the aid and insights of the following masters and teachers: Mister Lee Lozowick, Mister Gurdjieff, Madame de Salzmann, Mister E.J. Gold, Arnaud Desjardins, Osho Rajneesh, Sri Ramana Maharshi, J. Krishnamurti, Don Juan Matus (from Carlos Castaneda), Rodney Collin and others as noted in the book. (For the one-liners at the end of each chapter I am indebted to Jon Winokur. *Funny Times.* 28:6 [June 2013] 10).

Contents

Thema

You see, it is said in the ancient scriptures, "The mind is the slayer of the real." The constant functioning of the mind, the automatic thinking, prevents us from seeing reality. . . Krishnamurti says that our problem in the West is that we live either for the future, thinking of the future, or we think of the past. We never live in the now. If by some miracle we would live in the now, something could happen. But the mind interferes.

—Irina Tweedie, interview in
The Laughing Man 7:2, 49-50.

❦

There is surely nothing other than the single purpose of the present moment. A man's whole life is a succession of moment after moment. If one fully understands the present moment, there will be nothing else to do, and nothing else to pursue.

—from "Ghostdog: The Way of the Samurai," film by
Jim Jarmusch, 1999. Hagakure quote by Yamamoto Tsunetomi.

❦

I cannot say that I understand what it is to be present. This simply is not true, because I do not live it. When I live without being present, it means there is something I do not understand as I am (79). . . So, my effort is to remember myself. (81)

—Jeanne de Salzmann. *The Reality of Being*

Te Dominus Amat

Introduction

Here is an invitation to go on a journey. The destination of this journey is the present, to refocus one's Attention in the body, in the present moment, wherein all help resides. It is this struggle to maintain a present-Attention which may lead to inner growth and transformation. The development of Presence and Attention is the key to human life and to inner growth.

This book provides a map for the development of Presence and Attention. Such a map is useful only when I am finally, at last, willing to face and deal with the shock of seeing myself as I am. This seeing is difficult unless one has been prepared by long practice. I must see with complete clarity the hopelessness of my position, that I am helpless to bring about real, lasting change in myself as I am, that I cannot do anything about my position, and that every single effort I have ever made to change is useless. I must see and feel this fact and in order to avoid seeing and feeling this, I will seek any distraction, no matter how destructive or ludicrous. This seeing is the result of half of the Practice of Presence: self observation.

> [T]he dharma cannot be understood without a direct, personal relationship with a teacher...if teaching is to be genuine and alive, then personal contact with a teacher is vital.
> —Fabrice Midal. *Chögyam Trungpa:*
> *His Life and Vision, 44.*

Here a question arises for the reader: what if I don't have such a guide? This Work is not to be done in isolation, but with others, and preferably under the guidance of a wise teacher; the Master Jesus said, "Seek and ye shall find." In the absence of group or teacher, one begins the practice and holds the intention and the wish for help most sincerely in one's heart. Help will eventually come; this is the law when one holds sincere intention. When I am ready, a guide will arrive. I have a teacher, whom I call "guru." For me guru is both guide and a doorway to the Divine. Please do not be offended when I make such a connection. Whoever is just above you in understanding is guide for you. Help is lawful if one practices sincerely, which means honestly.

Moreover, you must not accept what is read here uncritically. *Verify everything* for yourself. Evaluate with your own personal experience. Otherwise, we all fall victim to our own worst tendencies. What is given here is the technology of transformation, not the experience. Your experience will be different from anyone else's, unique to you alone. Knowing what to do is knowledge; doing is wisdom. This book is meant to be used in conjunction with *Self Observation: The Awakening of Conscience.* Something old must die for something new to be born. That inner sacrifice can be difficult and painful. God bless you and protect you in your efforts. Lord have mercy. *Verify, verify, verify.*

Prologue

Placing Hope In What Is Permanent

Hope in the body is sickness and death;
it weakens as it ages and runs out of breath.

Hope in the mind is denial and madness;
it lies, steals our joy and ends in sadness.

Hope in the emotions is anger and fear;
they fight and flee love, waiting for a savior to appear.

Hope in Conscience is the doorway to the Divine;
not my will be done, but Thine.

Hope in consciousness develops the Soul;
there is no end to Its growth, the path is the goal.

Hope in conscious death leads me to conscious labor:
despite my flaws and his, I work to love my neighbor.

—Red Hawk

CHAPTER 1

Self Remembering:
The Practice of Presence

[He is] "talking about everyone 'being mostly disembodied,'
about not really having a body. Now how ridiculous is that?
... But suddenly I see what he's saying. Yeah, there's a body,
but I don't have a conscious awareness of it ... [He is] talking
again about redirecting the attention out of the head brain,
amping up the body's vibration, becoming embodied."

William Patrick Patterson, 221.

Remember yourself, seeker.

Self observation is absolutely essential if I wish to know myself and mature into a human being and not remain on the mammal level of existence—an unconscious, habit driven, *mechanical,**1 automatic-pilot slave to my personal history and to unconscious forces derived from that history (*see*: Red Hawk. *Self Observation: The Awakening of Conscience. An Owner's Manual*).

---

¹   Words marked with a star and italicized the first time they are used are defined in the Glossary at the end of the book.

Self observation and self remembering are not two separate practices; they are essential and bonded steps in the same practice. Self remembering must come first, then self observation may follow, as the seed must come before the plant can grow. Without self remembering, all so-called "self observation" is in the mind alone and therefore vulnerable to imagination and illusion, a part of the unconscious dreaming mechanism. Observation from the mind alone goes nowhere, produces fantasy and inner division, and may do harm or produce inner pathology. *The destination is the present—it must be constantly renewed with every breath or the connection is lost.*

Self remembering places the observer in time and space, in the present, in the body, grounds the observation in the body. The present is the destination for *work on self.** Unless the body is brought into play in self observation, the practice goes nowhere. At its most fundamental level, first-stage self remembering is remembering that I *have* a body and exist for a time *in* this body: "I am here now."

Self observation from the mind alone can result in harmful pathology. Every spiritual path has a pathology. One pathology associated with self observation is a self-centered self-obsession (which is why the practice of self remembering involves not just self, but the other). I wish to work *with* the mind, not *from* the mind. Working from, or in, the mind alone produces a schism, an inner separation whereby I begin to judge and work against what I observe, rather than *with* what is observed and *for* my inner aims.* I fight with what is observed, under the delusion that I can change what I see. This fight to change what is observed produces wrong results, often harmful, and leads me in a wrong direction from which I may never recover.

As I come to know myself as a mechanical entity, taken constantly in *identification** with the mechanical habits of the body, I begin to develop a body of conscious impressions whose accumulation builds both *will** and *wish** in me so that I do not forget my habitual unconsciousness. This accumulation of impressions provides a force behind my wish to remain present. Only then will my resistance to being taken by habit help me see and feel my slavery more.

Split Attention

But self remembering has another aspect to it which is quite unusual among all of the world's spiritual paths: self remembering, as Mister Gurdjieff taught us, means to split one's Attention, directing one portion of it toward, and including, the surrounding external environment, or the person in front of whom I stand, and the other portion of the Attention is directed onto myself—at the same time—so that I not only listen to, and am aware of, the other but I am aware of myself listening.

Attention is in the body, and on the body in the form of *sensation,** while it is also on the external environment. Madame Jeanne de Salzmann (Gurdjieff's senior student and the author of *The Reality of Being: The Fourth Way of Gurdjieff*) gives this ratio: 75 percent Attention inward, 25 percent Attention external. This quality of split Attention is only possible with conscious labor—it does not, cannot, occur mechanically or by accident. It is what is meant, on one level, by conscious labor. Just as the placement of Attention at the solar plexus or abdominal region is a conscious move, and is the most fundamental level of self remembering, so too is the splitting of Attention, which is second-stage self remembering.

Placement of Attention Is Destiny

What I place my Attention on, I become. This is a law. It is the law of identification. Conscious placement of Attention escapes the law of identification and places me under the laws of *the Work*.* We are governed by laws of a higher and lower order. Our work is to place ourselves under the influence of those higher laws.

Conscious Attention is different from automatic, mechanical attention, which we are born with. Conscious Attention must be developed consciously. Attention is the key to this and to human life on Earth. The *Being** is Presence and Attention, nothing more nor less. *Consciousness*,* which is God, is the field in which all phenomena arise. Attention is consciousness localized and focused on a specific point in that field. That field is sensitive and aware, ultimately capable of being aware of itself as consciousness, which is the most mature form of self remembering. The *soul*,* or Being, has two essential qualities: Presence and Attention. Souls are sent to Earth to develop as Presence and Attention. The struggle to be present develops both Presence and Attention. Self remembering invokes Presence; self observation invokes Attention. The struggle to be present allows me to observe the self in action. It begins with the struggle to remember the body and consciously place Attention *in* the body, moving it out of the mind and down, below the neck. This moves Attention out of identification with the thoughts in the intellectual *center*,* the cause of the great majority of our suffering. Thus, it is the most fundamental level of self remembering.

But this struggle to be present is not so simple; it appears easy, but in fact is nearly impossible to do. I cannot remain present in the *now* of the body for more than a few seconds, but then I have an inner reaction to impressions and I am taken in identification with thought or emotion at once. This is because being present in the body is a different state of consciousness than I have been accustomed to. It is the waking state. It takes a long time to become accustomed to this new, higher state of consciousness. I do not see that Attention is taken by identification for a long time. I believe that I am present. Continued self observation reveals otherwise. What is more, I do not see that I *want* to be taken, because the fear of seeing the horror of my real inner state is overwhelming and I would rather be distracted, constantly. I cannot remain present because Presence and Attention are both weak in me; they are not developed. That is why I am given a body: to develop these two things which are the essential qualities of the "*I-am** Being" within. The body is an *objective** feedback mechanism meant to orient the Being in the present. The destination of the Work is the present; one of the aims of the Work is to develop Presence and Attention to the point where they are stable enough to withstand the shock of physical death of the body and remain present, without being scattered and taken in identification. We work in life to practice our dying.

Formatory Apparatus

Mind, as we ordinarily know and use it, is memory—or what Mister Gurdjieff calls "formatory apparatus." There is more to mind than this, of course; only ten percent of the left hemisphere is memory function and this is "the thinker." So when I say "mind" it is a very restricted and specific function, this thinker of which I speak.

The thinker, as we know it, is memory, the storehouse of my personal history. All thought (not inspiration or intuition, which are higher intellectual and emotional functions and are another order of thinking entirely) is memory recalling personal history. All thought is from the known, which is the past, or personal history.

The thinker and the thought are the same (J. Krishnamurti). So all self observation which comes from mind alone is the thinker observing itself, judging what it sees, and trying to change itself, based only and exclusively on what is known: the past, personal history. Thus, there is only repetition of habit, doing the same things and hoping for different results. This is insanity.

Unless I can observe from a place *outside* the mind, I can only repeat the same old habits and see nothing. I am blind to myself, one portion of the mind judging another portion of the mind—a self divided, another definition of insanity. Self remembering gives me the possibility of conscious placement of Attention in the body, below the mind, from which I may observe the mind more objectively.

All judgment is from the mind. Judgment is a strategy to avoid relationship, and the first relationship has to be with the body; otherwise no relationship is possible. Eventually, self observation will reveal to me that, as it is formed in our society, the mind is separated from the body, a self divided. There is this separation in me.

The mind is a liar, not by intention—because it is a computer, without volition—but by its very nature and structure. It cannot be believed because it distorts reality to fit its own habitual patterns, based on my personal history. We have been conditioned in such a way that the mind is made to run the body and therefore my life, all alone; this demand is given over to the memory function. This function is a binary computer—mechanical and unconscious. The demand to operate the life of the body all alone overwhelms the mind. It is not created to do such an enormous task; therefore, it must become a generalization machine.

Neuroscientists estimate that the mind receives about two billion discrete bits of information per second. It is impossible for it to process this massive amount of impressions. They estimate that mind is capable of processing about 2,000 discrete bits of information per second, or roughly .001 percent of the impressions which compose our reality. On what basis does the mind select this .001 percent to catalog and store? Simple. It selects based on my personal history, what is known (memory), what it recognizes and can easily categorize and store.

Thus, the mind is a generalization machine—it must generalize these incoming impressions because they come at a rate far too rapid to sort and catalog. So this generalizing function is unconscious and mechanical; it is done based on that incoming data which supports and validates the mind's already existing patterns. Try to intuit—without thinking about it—what this may mean.

I am only receiving from the mind that data from external reality which supports and validates those mental and emotional patterns set in place from earliest childhood, placed there by unconscious caregivers who enacted those received patterns which came from *their* caregivers, and it goes back and back: ingrained family pathologies repeated generation after generation, unconsciously and without any awareness.

The mind is a liar because it is programmed to be so. Any data that is received from external reality and does not support or validate those ingrained patterns is automatically rejected, ignored, or distorted so that it is made to fit the patterns of the intellectual-emotional complex.

The Fear Factory

Now I may see clearly one simple fact, which must be verified by one's own observation: the mind is a "fear factory" (Mister Gurdjieff), and because I identify deeply with it, I live in terror. The mind as it is now is a strategic tool to distract the essential Being, to capture Attention so that it avoids seeing and feeling the horror which is "myself." It does so by constant, relentless thought, judging and naming every single thing both inside, what I call "myself," and outside. Mammal life, life as I know it in ordinary mammal reality—life that is unconscious, mechanical—is made up nearly exclusively of distractions (E. J. Gold). Distractions are the fabric of ordinary reality. I am taken by them because I fear seeing the horror of my real inner state.

The mind is a generalization machine, as noted above. Because it is asked to perform an impossible task—control of the body and the life, and therefore all relationships—it must generalize about everything, creating categories which easily allow it to recognize and store incoming impressions by association, comparison and contrast. Thus, it does the easiest possible thing: it creates two large, all-encompassing categories of information into which it places all impressions: like–dislike. Or call it love–hate, or black–white, or *Aha!*, good–evil. Now can you intuit what the Biblical parable (or allegory or metaphor) of the Garden of Eden means? It is meant to describe the law of identification and what that means for a human being when Attention is captured, captivated, and fascinated (identified) with the movement of the mind, the intellectual center, the "Tree of Knowledge." It is a warning. Beware! If I "eat of the fruit of the Tree of Knowledge of Good and Evil" (the mind), I will be cast out of Paradise (the Garden, the body, the present), and know shame. I will be ashamed that I am naked, and cover myself to hide my nakedness—I will lose my "organic innocence" (Lee Lozowick). I cover myself with constant, obsessive distractions and with the creation of what I call "myself."

Can you intuit—without thinking about it—why self remembering is such a crucial function in the practice of self observation; why the body must be brought into play before I can observe truthfully and objectively? Unless Attention is consciously shifted from the mind to the body, only lies can occur. Reality will be distorted, and I will only perceive what the mind is conditioned to see—my personal history and the patterns resulting from that history. It cannot be otherwise. What self observation eventually reveals is that what I know and call "myself" is a collection of memories: my personal history, stored in the memory function. The mental computer can only perceive what it is programmed to perceive. Thus it is, and can only be, a liar when it is asked to do more than it was created to do. What is that?

The mind has four primary functions, which it is very able and effective at performing:

1) solving technical problems in the present (how to fasten my shoes, how to get home from here, how to plan my day's activities);

2) communicating with others;

3) remembering;

4) serving Presence and Attention.

Thus, the mind plays a crucial function in self remembering: I must remember my practice with the help of the mind; thus, it serves. Once it remembers, its job is finished. Now a conscious volition must take over, from the Being, and Attention must consciously shift to the body, where self observation can take place.

Fear Separates / Love Unites

The mind is a binary computer. What that means is simply that it breaks everything down into two parts (the two generalized categories noted above): like–dislike. It does that with *everything*, including relationships. Can you intuit what this may mean for your relationships?

The mind separates and divides all information, all experiences, all reality, into two parts. Fear separates and divides; love unites. Thus, the unconscious operation of the mind is the operation of fear overlaying received reality, organizing it into recognizable patterns based on its stored personal history, and recognizing *only* that data which supports and validates those fearful patterns. It insists on maintaining the status quo, no matter how damaging, harmful, painful or even life threatening that status quo may be. *Suck cigarette smoke, even though it will likely kill the body?* Sure, just so long as it supports preexisting patterns, which means those patterns which support how I feel about myself and about my life. The unconscious operation of the mind is fear. Therefore, everything which it recognizes and chooses to validate as real is fear-based. It cannot be otherwise, because its fundamental operating principle is fear.

Therefore, if the mind is binary, it operates on relationship exactly as it operates on all received reality: it is fear, categorizing and generalizing—lying—about love. Fear blocks love. More precisely, fear is the absence of love, just as darkness is the absence of light. Fear has no qualities of its own; it exists only as the absence of a positive quality. It is the shadow of reality, not reality itself. And because the mind is binary, it breaks relationship, love, down into two parts, which automatically, by its very nature, destroys love.

Love unites; fear divides. Fear is the absence of love. When I am attracted to someone, the mind generalizes this attraction and stores it in the like–dislike categories. It very quickly begins to make a list about the other person: *here is what I like about him, here is what I dislike.* And can you intuit which list gets longer and longer, and therefore comes to dominate Attention? And can you further intuit what the result for the relationship is, even if we stay together?

Perhaps you have enough experience with this phenomenon to appreciate what this means for your life. My personal history is littered, like a battlefield after war, with the corpses of failed relationships which have been operated upon by the mind. The result is predictable and inevitable, because the mind is a judgment machine which operates on generalizations: "He is always . . . (fill in)" or "I hate it when she always . . . (fill in)." All judgments are a strategy to avoid relationship because they are fear-based.

Self remembering must come first; then self observation follows. Where there is judgment, no self observation is possible. Judgment comes from identification ("I am that") and is fear-based. Love never judges. Fear judges. *Non-judgmental love** is conscious love, the love of the Being (soul) which is mature Presence and Attention. Mature Attention only observes without speaking, naming, categorizing, or judging. Mature Attention is "witness consciousness" or "silent witness," which is consciousness aware of itself and expanded to include all of reality, excluding nothing, including all. This is the most mature level, the third stage, of self remembering. Non-judgmental love includes all, excludes none. Our *Creator** is non-judgmental love.

No Right Way

It is useful to sound this note of caution right at the beginning: there is no single or "right" way to the practice of self remembering. It is infinite in its variety and possibilities; it is unique to each individual practitioner. What follows in this book are some useful guidelines and suggestions for beginning this practice, but they are not final words by some so-called expert. They are suggestions from a practitioner like yourself: a mechanic and not a guru or a master; a beginner, not an adept. This book only introduces the practice of self remembering, hints at its possibilities, and suggests a few fundamental ways of looking at it. It is not exhaustive, nor is it an authority. In all things spiritual, you must verify for yourself, never taking the word of another in place of your own personal experience.

I'm [so] paranoid [that] on my stationary bike I have a rear-view mirror.

—Richard Lewis

A BRIEF NOTE TO THE READER: I am aware that I repeat myself in this book, stating and then later re-stating information which I have gone over before. There are several reasons for this. The first is that this information threatens the *ego*,* which moves rapidly to ignore, discredit, or eliminate it from its memory-function because *it does not support and validate its patterns;* so from one chapter to the next, a reader is likely to forget everything which was said in the preceding chapter, by unconscious design of the binary computer. It is designed to ignore that data which does not support its hard-earned and desperately important categories and patterns. The second reason, closely following the first, is that the information herein contained needs to be repeated over and over *in order to retain it for use in my practice.* The *Practice of Presence** is self remembering/self observation—they are not two separate practices, but a single unified practice. I cannot observe myself unless and until I remember myself. First I remember, then I observe.

Thus. Very well, I repeat myself. Perhaps you may intuit why now, and not allow the judgments of the mind to disturb your focus of Attention on the material at hand.

A Vigilant Man Guards His Home

The body is our home, but we spend our whole
    lives
in slavery to it, laboring long hours at work
we mostly hate, for what? To feed, clothe,
and shelter the body. We spend our life force,
that precious breath, on a mind which gives
itself to desire and goes mad, utterly berserk
with an unending thirst for more, and is loathe
to yield to the smallest discipline, like a horse

who has taken the bit and run over a cliff,
taking us with it to our inevitable doom.
Life lived in insatiable desire is grief,
robs us of dignity, leaves us empty and undone.
A vigilant man guards his home against that thief,
never sleeps, keeps a watchful eye on every room.

—Red Hawk. *Mother Guru*, 63

CHAPTER 2

Spiritual Surgery:
The Removal of Self-importance

What weakens us is feeling offended by the deeds and misdeeds of other men. Our self-importance requires that we spend most of our lives offended by someone. Without self-importance we are invulnerable.
—Carlos Castaneda, *The Fire from Within*, 12.

Self remembering, and self remembering only, thus enables a man to shed the outer skin of personality and to feel and act freely from his essence, that is to be himself. In this way he may separate himself from the pretences and imitations which have enslaved him since childhood, and return to what he actually is, return to his own essential nature.
—Rodney Collin, *The Theory of Celestial Influence*, 230.

Some who come to the school are overcome by grief; some by yearning; some by sadness; still others by hope. All these are simply burdens carried in from the dream. Conditioning is burned away through friction and self-remembering.
—E. J. Gold, *The Joy of Sacrifice*, 89.

When my spiritual Master Mister Lee gave me the task of writing the book *Self Observation* I believed that once I delivered the finished manuscript it was exactly that: finished. It was not. It was the beginning of a new *work octave** which I could never have imagined or foreseen. It was, to put it in its most dramatic terms, a death sentence. What I now see very clearly is that putting my name to such a book called for a level of personal responsibility, personal integrity, and work on self which was far beyond my own ability to manage, at that time, and which placed me directly in the Master's fire.

I have been asked to speak on the practice of self observation in public gatherings. I have done so, and the extraordinary events which have followed this exercise, for me personally, have been astonishing. Ever since the first experience of writing the book, Mister Lee has delivered a series of shocks to me, a whole chain of them, literally one after the other and unrelenting, which have served to expose my self-importance and its effect on self and on those who come into contact with me. I have been willing to see and feel what these shocks have laid bare, and the suffering, the horror really, has been most intense *sadhana* (spiritual practice; the path to awakening) for me. What Mister Lee has done is to surgically remove my *buffer** system so that I cannot—and do not wish to—hide from what is being shown me.

My *guru** is protecting me, and those he brings me into contact with, from the body of habits which would destroy my work, given the work demands now being placed upon me, unless a self-correcting mechanism, such as self remembering and self observation provide, was allowed to do its work in me. The guru in his mercy has surgically exposed that in me which would do the most harm to me personally, and to those who have sought me out for feedback and support in their own practice of self observation.

What I now see is my inner brittleness, my insensitivity to others—a lack of compassion, the absence of kindness, the illusion that I know something—and behind it all is the fear that I am no good, my lack of self-worth. And behind that still, which self observation has shown me, is my primal fear: fear of abandonment. I was adopted as an infant. My fear is covered by a transparent bluff, a loud illusion of certainty. I live in terror.

Fear and Longing

Because of the elegance of Mister Lee's surgery upon my self-importance, two things have resulted in me: 1) fear of my self-importance; 2) longing.

Many years ago I read this quote from Madame Ouspensky which troubled me when I read it and which created in me the illusion that I understood what she meant:

> *All work is based on watchfulness. The man who works realizes he is a machine and fears his machine. Therefore he watches. While there is a guardian at the door those who go in and out can be scrutinized . . . a healthy cell does this work by itself.*
> —Talks By Madame Ouspensky, 1.

This little booklet just quoted, long out of print, contains the profound shock that the more I see my mechanicalness, my habitual reactions to impressions, the more I come to fear the unconscious operation of the machine, the body of habits. I have come to that fear. My self-importance is exposed daily from unexpected directions, and it does not relent, despite repeated exposures. Therefore, I must watch. I am compelled by this fear of its effects upon others and on me, the pain it causes them and me, to remain more vigilant than I have ever been in my life. Why? Because the pain of its effects is unbearable: *intentional suffering.* *

I fear what I am capable of when I am unconscious. I live in what Mister Gurdjieff called "the terror of the situation." I see that when I identify with certain "I's" in me, I am capable of anything, any level of harm, and I am helpless; my life is unmanageable. Therefore, I have urgency to work. I have the necessity of radical reliance upon the guru and God.

---

* While I am deeply indebted to Mister Gurdjieff, and I make use of most of his terminology in speaking of the practice of Presence, still I am not bound to that terminology. In the first volume of this exploration of the practice of self remembering/self observation, entitled *Self Observation: The Awakening of Conscience,* I have changed "intentional suffering" to "voluntary suffering" for the simple reason that this change allows us to approach this practice from a different angle. It is accessible in a way which is slightly more descriptive of the process; thus it is more readily comprehended by an untrained audience. However, I am aware of the distinction which Mister Gurdjieff makes between "intentional" and "voluntary" in his 3rd Series, *Life Is Real Only Then, When 'I Am.'* Here He says,

> When he came, in the translation, to the expression used by me, 'intentional suffering,' I interrupted his reading, for he had translated the word 'intentional' by the word 'voluntary.'

> As I attempted to explain the great difference between the voluntary and intentional suffering of man, there arose a general philological discussion, as is usual in such cases. (151)

Thus, in the present volume I have reverted to Mister Gurdjieff's preferred terminology, with a bow to his wisdom and to his level of understanding, which is not my own. Terminology is a map; one does not want to get bound to the map, but to use it as a reference point while exploring the territory. Any change in terminology arises from my exploration of the territory, feet on the ground, and not because I think I know more, or better, than others.

The Sufis have a great teaching: "Be not absent for the length of a single breath." What once seemed like an impossible ideal has now become, for me, an impossible necessity. I cannot do it by myself. Only surrender to my Master makes such a thing even worth considering. He brings daily shock to my self observation, which serves as a constant source of remorse, my self-centered insensitivity to others, as well as to myself. This remorse, which goes so deeply, piercing the innermost heart of Being, has become a most valuable inner reminding factor which helps me to be more awake. I am afraid to sleep. I cannot afford it. And still I sleep. Madame Ouspensky continues:

> *A man who knows what is profitable will not steal from himself but saves his energy, knowing that nothing can come without energy . . . To be collected in oneself is essential, but it is necessary to be collected in the right place [my emphasis. RH] . . . One must be relaxed to be properly collected. One must hold on nowhere.*
>
> —Talks. 1.

Lee, by his kind grace, has allowed me to see my self-importance so clearly that I fear it. This fear is his grace alone. I see how self-importance steals from me and steals from my relationships—it is a strategy to avoid relationship in fact. In the absence of this energy within, I am unable to remember myself, and thus to observe myself. I am an unconscious mechanism, a creature who is habit driven. I live a creature life, not the life of a human being, and all of my relationships reflect this.

But the second thing which has arisen from my Master's subtle surgery is a deep longing. And this longing, when coupled with the fear of sleep, can bring about transformation. The longing is simply this: to remember myself, always and in everything. Furthermore, I long to stop avoiding relationship both within myself and with others. I long for an end to my imagined separation from our Creator, which means in simple terms that I long to be always and everywhere present in the *now* of the body.

This is what is meant by the above-mentioned Sufi teaching: "Be not absent for the length of a single breath." This is no longer a theory for me. It is a compelling urgency, a necessity if I am to represent my Master's teaching in the way that he is asking of me. It is, at least at my present level of awareness, an impossibility, and yet breath is one major ally in fulfilling this aim. So the Sufis point to the breath as essential in this aim. Thus, when Madame Ouspensky emphasized that I must be "collected in the right place," this is perhaps one of the ways I may understand this directive. Self remembering, for me, involves the sensing of the breath. Placing Attention on the breath helps me to "be collected in the right place." But I must endure the slow accumulation of impressions, and accompanying shocks, when I see myself as I am, in order to not forget what I am and remain "collected in the right place." As I am now, I have not accumulated enough force of Attention to remain in place for very long before I am distracted by inner reaction to impressions. But the interval between Presence and absence grows ever shorter because of this conscious accumulation of impressions. I return more often, and remain longer.

The Bodily Location of Objectivity

Another way I may utilize this teaching of Madame Ouspensky's is to experiment with and test for myself the conscious placement of Attention in the body; that is, to locate in myself a place from which I might observe the self more objectively, without judgment, which means without identification with what is observed.

There are a few possibilities for this placement, and according to what spiritual school I find myself in, that bodily location of objectivity may vary. For myself, and following the various hints of Mister Gurdjieff, well buried and scattered in his writings, I have settled upon the abdominal area of the solar plexus as a starting point. I have experimented with various locations. You must find your own place by trial and error. But one thing is certain: in order to observe the mind objectively, it must be from a position outside of the mind. I cannot observe "the first ring of power" (the mind) from within that ring; Attention must be placed consciously in what Carlos Castaneda has called "the second ring of power" (which is down lower in the body, below the neck) in order to observe that first ring. This requires a "shift in the assemblage point" (that point in the body where one's view of reality is assembled—in most of us, this is in the mind. Again this is Castaneda's term. Some would locate this point outside the physical body, in the "energy body" which surrounds the physical body. For our purposes in this investigation, I will locate this point in the physical body). It requires a conscious shift of Attention to a new bodily location. Otherwise I go round in circles, getting nowhere, with no transformation possible.

Why We Pray

The fear produces this prayer in me: "Lord, have mercy."
The longing produces this prayer in me: "I wish to work."

It is absurd to pretend in my sleep that I wish to work, while all the time dreaming that I can.
    —Jeanne de Salzmann, *The Reality of Being*, 78.

As my friend in the Work Lee Van Laer says, at this stage of one's work there are only three practices: "Prayer, prayer, and more prayer."

The suffering which I am now experiencing at the kind and generous hands of my Master is grateful suffering, is suffering not of the ordinary mechanical kind, but a deeper, long-sought-after type of *conscious suffering.** He is putting me into place and I am undergoing what I call "the humbling process" by his grace. But this suffering is intense, painful, and difficult—mitigated and gracefully endured by humor. It demands everything from me in terms of inner work. It is often raging and mad. It is at times physically painful and emotionally devastating. It is a "dark night of the soul" which has lasted for months and months. But there is also the aim to not take myself so seriously, to find good humor in the situation, and to laugh at myself. At times the "terror of the situation" is overwhelming. There were times when I thought I would die. I could not get a full breath without great effort. My heart raced. I awoke at night in a cold sweat. I could eat very little. I wanted to live curled into a fetal ball. So the question finally and naturally arises in this work, at this stage of *purification of the centers:** Am I willing to die doing this work?

My decision has been, better to get it over with in this lifetime than to carry it over into the next. And to get over myself, my self dramatization, and self-importance.

I have prayed for humility for a long time. I did not expect this was how it would come, with such deep intensity and suffering and fear and longing. But my Master knows; I do not know. I see clearly in this surgical process my own nothingness, helplessness, and also clearly what Mister Gurdjieff teaches as "I cannot 'do.'" My Osho sangha-brother Maitreya, an Advaita spiritual

teacher in his own right, has this to say about the suffering which
I now endure:

> *The sense of being an individual doer is programmed into*
> *every ego's structure. The ego-doer is needed to create the*
> *illusion of separation that manifests as suffering in humans.*
> *Separation and suffering provide the essential contrast to*
> *the ecstasy of enlightenment . . . Understanding this concept*
> *of grace as divine will free you from any kind of need to*
> *achieve anything . . . Human helplessness and vulnerability*
> *apply equally to enlightened ones, but they have adjusted*
> *to the reality of surrender . . . Hence Buddhas enjoy life free*
> *from suffering.*
>
> —Maitreya, via email

Another of the Sufis' great and valuable teachings is this:
"Only good will come of this." It does not matter what "this" is.
This is a very high teaching indeed. It is the teaching of surrender
to the will of God, the grace of the guru. It is a teaching of faith in
the goodness and perfection of the Master's world.

Thus, as I lay on my Master's operating table—without benefit of anesthesia but with trust in his *dharma*—I am left with
"Just This" (Mister Lee): "accepting what is, as it is, here and now"
(Arnaud Desjardins). I am left with the *now* of the body consciously
relaxed, as it is being surgically operated upon—an "ego-ectomy."

And finally, this is my prayer: "Lord have mercy; I wish to
work." My Master has broken me. He has broken my heart so
deeply and thoroughly that only God can heal me. Heartbreak of
this order can only be seen as a gift of mercy and grace, arising
from consciously placing myself in the position to receive help
from above. I am bathed in sorrow and drowned in tears (Irina

Tweedie). I place myself in the now, which is the Sacred Heart of Mercy. Lord have mercy; I wish to work.

This prayer makes possible what was once impossible. One of Chögyam Trungpa Rinpoche's highest teachings was this: "If kindness doesn't work, try more kindness." This prayer ("Lord have mercy; I wish to work") is a prayer for the courage, the patience, and the compassion to put this highest practice into play in my relationships. Self-importance, in even its most subtle manifestations, makes such a practice impossible. And yet I cannot simply drop self-importance. It is not that easy. In fact, it is impossible. Only grace can excise self-importance. The work is to allow this surgery to take place. How? By conscious placement of Attention so that one is "collected in the right place," and by conscious relaxation of the body so that the surgeon has access to it and may perform his miracle. One may view this "surgeon" as one's practice and as the lawful result of such practice.

The Suffering of Transformation

The surgery is not fast, nor is it easy to bear. It is surgically precise and it is tailored to the needs, the level of practice, the level of Being, and the ability of the patient to endure the intervention of the Divine into the human life. It is dependent upon surrender, in other words. And that surrender depends upon how much, and for how long, one is able to endure observing self-importance and its effects, both externally and internally.

How much suffering am I willing to endure, for the sake of the work of my Master? That has been my ongoing question. One might also put it this way: How much suffering am I willing to endure for the sake of restoring my original sanity and wholeness?

And this level of self observation depends upon both a sense of humor and the ability to remember myself, always and in everything, as Mister Gurdjieff says. Without self remembering, no real work is possible. The struggle to remain present in the *now* of the body develops Presence and Attention, those essential aspects of Being. Self remembering invokes Presence; self observation invokes Attention. As they develop, one is able to remain for longer periods of time in the suffering of transformation. Suffering in this sense is not a negative term; it is one aspect of the positive process of transformation, without which this process cannot go on. One suffers in order to be transformed by our Creator. Seeing and feeling myself *as I am* is intentional suffering in order to grow and mature as a Being.

And I do not remember myself. So my Master provides me with suffering brought on by my self-importance. This helps me remember myself. Do you see the beauty of this that I am now caught up in? Do you see how prayers are answered? Lord have mercy; I wish to work.

We have heard it a hundred times in the sleeping media: be careful what you wish for. Wish has power, when it is held consciously in the heart. Wish is mother to aim. My wish is to work; my aim is to remember myself, always and in everything—to not be absent for the length of a single breath. In order to fulfill the wishes of my Master, I must be surgically altered. In the vessel as it is presently constructed, with its multitude of energetic leaks in the form of distractions, among which is self-importance, I cannot hold the energy which is required to do the Master's work in the world.

This idea of self-importance takes many forms. For example, for me, in this book, there is always the danger of coming across as one who knows something you don't know, the danger of presenting oneself as being right while others are not, and the trap of appearing superior and certain in one's opinions, presenting opinion as fact. Then there is the opposite side of the coin: the assumption and declaration that I am inferior, ignorant, neurotic and full of flaws, which is self-importance masquerading as self-hatred.

I wish to consciously, voluntarily, place myself upon the operating table. I wish to remember myself. Then my work is single-pointed: keep Attention collected in the proper place and keep the body consciously relaxed (this is also the work of the woman giving birth) as the surgeon does his work.

One must pay for what one is given; this is the law of the Work. And the greater the gift, the more one must pay with the dearest coin in one's purse: self-importance. Something must die for something to be born. This is what I call "the humbling process." This is what I call "the religion of the *now* of the body." *Now* is the only religion; everything else is imagination. The guru's domain is now. The now of the body is the domain in which the Divine, the surgeon, operates; it is the realm of transformation. The body exists as an objective feedback mechanism to help orient the Being in the present, *here now*, which is the only place and the only way in which it can develop.

What This Practice May Reveal

I have not always been willing to undertake such a difficult and demanding practice as self remembering. It requires that I see and feel myself exactly as I am, with ruthless self honesty, to accumulate impressions so that I do not so easily forget. This is hard work, which is why it is called "the Work." It demands total sacrifice of that which is most precious and well-defended: the suffering of an individual and separate self. One is called upon to sacrifice suffering and surrender it to the wisdom and gentle transformations of non-judgmental love, our Creator. One is called upon to give up all seeking and relax into the *now* of the body of love. One is asked to stop interfering with the will of "God as love."

I am willing to engage such a radical transformative practice only because years of self observation have revealed to me the following: 1) I am enslaved by unconscious forces, mechanical urges, and repetitive habits; 2) I am helpless before them; 3) I am incapable of meaningful, lasting change alone; 4) I cannot hold Attention in place for very long before it gets lost in identification; 5) I have lived most of my life in the hell of the separative, self-centered, and self-important ego; 6) and I have seen its effect on all of my relationships.

The simplest definition of hell is this: no love. No love is hell. I have seen deeply into the hell I have created, unconsciously and mechanically, by identification with the intellectual-emotional complex. Now I wish to align myself with a different but not separate force in me: the will of God as love. This wish must be fueled by the conscious accumulation of impressions (Madame de Salzmann).

This alignment with the will of God must be done consciously. It cannot be otherwise—I cannot align with consciousness unconsciously. That is common sense. To be conscious is to be objective about the arising of all phenomena, inner and outer; to take no position regarding the arising of phenomena, inner and outer; and to not identify with the mechanics of the body's world.

My spiritual Master Mister Lee said, "A life of elegance is a life without complaint." That means non-identification with arising phenomena. The Sufis were right: "Only good will come of this," no matter what "this" is.

I see myself as I am, unable to hold Attention in place for long, subject to indulgence of all kinds, and identified with various "i's" in me. All I have to offer God is a willingness to work and serve. I offer God this self, exactly as it is. I lay myself before the feet of the guru/God as a conscious offering, as food, to be consumed in love. God or Love must do the rest. I practice, It works.

In order to allow God as love to change me, "I" must become sensation-Attention only. I can't work from the mind. I must become my work. "I" must become sensation-Attention—sensation from the body, Attention from the Being—a perfect marriage within, a union instead of a separation. What is called for is a life of meditation lived in the now of the body as God, and the stillness of the Being.

I am not long for this world, so I practice as if my death depended on it. It does.

Neurotic means he is not as sensible as I am, and psychotic means he's even worse than my brother-in-law.

—Karl Menninger

The Death of A Conscious Man
(*Mister Lee*)

i. His beauty is infused in the world,
the sea heaves,
there is a trembling in the leaves,
all the banners of the grasses unfurl.
Adore. Adore.

There are only dry eyes at our table;
we laugh at death's feeble efforts
to claim what it is unable to seize,
what slips its grasp with ease.

He never repeats Himself.
He flies south to His Father, a sweet
soft song on His lips;
He cheats death and yet

His humility is endless.
　　If you see a new star in the night sky
where none ever was before,
it is my Master.
Adore. Adore.

ii. We tie our women to the bedpost
or they would throw themselves
naked into the burning sky, nipples straining,
yearning to be nearer to the Holy Ghost.
Adore. Adore.

His absence fills the space, stuns every room
into silence, moves like a bad dream
through a troubled sleep. Nothing is as it seems,
everyone is broken by the impending doom

of the torn and ravaged flesh and bone.
I am an old man alone, deafened
by the silence which remains
after you have left this world bereft.

Though you are gone, you alone remain;
the joy of the wind sings your pure delight.
Happiness is all you want from us;
what else are we here for?
Adore. Adore.

—Red Hawk. *Mother Guru*, 40

CHAPTER 3

Separation Grief:
The Terror of the Situation
—Self Remembering: First Stage—

A human who does not bond with the Earth goes crazy.
—Oyate Shunkawakan Waste. Lakota Sioux Shaman

He who sees the diverse forms of life all rooted in the One, and growing forth from Him, he shall indeed find the Absolute. (131)

The saints with great effort find Him within themselves; but not the unintelligent, who in spite of every effort cannot control their minds. (141)

That knowledge which sees the One Indestructible in all beings, the One Indivisible in all separate lives, may be truly called Pure Knowledge. (164)

And when he becomes one with the Eternal, and his soul knows the bliss that belongs to the Self, he feels no desire and no regret, he regards all beings equally and enjoys the blessing of supreme devotion to Me. (170)

—*The Bhagavad Gita.*

The human race, being one mass mind, is on a suicide course. It does not have the power to destroy the Earth; the Earth will survive humanity. But humanity is set on destroying the Earth's ability to support human life. We have poisoned the Earth's atmosphere: the air we breathe is seriously contaminated from discharge all over the planet; the water we drink is toxically contaminated by industrial heavy metals and other discharge, from toxic chemical farm-runoff, and from human waste of all kinds; the soil we grow our food in has been destroyed by heavier and heavier doses of sprayed insecticides, herbicides, and pesticides which kill all life forms in the soil, including micro-organisms which break down soil nutrients and allow fine root hairs of plants to absorb them, and also including earthworms which aerate the soil; then the soil is heavily dosed with nitrogen-rich fertilizers to compensate for the damage so that crops can grow. The result is dead soil artificially juiced which produces food that has been robbed of its nutritional value.

The human race is a mass mind. The mind of the race is exactly like the individual mind, which was described in Chapter 1. It is an unconscious, mechanical, deluded mind which is fear-based. We live in the age of terror, because that is the world which this mind has created in its own image. The race will continue to do exactly as it has always done, which is to act selfishly and blindly, unconsciously, distracting its attention from reality and acknowledging only that data which supports and validates its preexisting patterns, no matter how destructive or deadly those patterns may be. It cannot do otherwise. The mind is a status-quo machine. It is strategically programmed to avoid relationship.

Because all their strategies are intact, worked out in reaction
to the parental situation, people dramatize their early-life

*oedipal strategies in the ordinary social or political circum-
stance of daily life even into old age.*
> —Da Free John. "Killing the Tiger."
> *Laughing Man* 7:2. 17.

Humanity is on a suicide course for one simple reason: it suffers from separation grief and separation anxiety. Any animal separated from its mother-matrix suffers separation grief and separation anxiety. It leads a life of sorrow and fear. It goes crazy. That is the state of the human race, governed by its single mass mind. Any efforts to correct this situation on a large scale are doomed to fail, because the problem is being addressed by the very mind which not only has caused the problem, but which *is* the problem. The mass mind always operates at the level of the lowest common denominator. The situation can only be corrected on the level of the individual.

And to address the problem on the individual level, the first requirement is that I remember myself. I must consciously place the self in time and space, in my immediate surroundings: "I am here now, in this body, in this place." This is first-stage self remembering. In a further refinement, a second stage, I become conscious not only of my inner movements, but also of my surroundings and my place in them. At the same time that I am aware of myself, I become aware of those beings, both human and animal and plant, which are in my immediate environment, and I act in a manner toward them with what is needed and wanted, what is appropriate to the situation. One considers others as well as oneself. In so doing, one avoids selfish, self-obsessed pathology. Thus, in the mature Being-state of a conscious Being, one places others before oneself. One considers what is in the best interest of the other before one's own well-being. This is the nature of non-judgmental love.

However, humans suffer from separation grief. We are separated from, have lost our feeling for, have failed to bond with, our natural mother the Earth, and by extension with the human body, which is of the Earth, comes from the Earth, and returns to the Earth when it is used up. When this happens, all beings go crazy. Witness the animals in the zoo who pace constantly in a state of madness, or lie comatose in a state of lethargy from which they cannot rise.

But our craziness comes much closer than that. In my present state, I live separated from my own body. I live in a state which is identified with the mind, and the mind separates itself from the body. Mind and body are not joined, are not unified, are not in harmony. The result is neuroses of all kinds and psychoses, madness. In the life of the mind, the species and the individual both act from personal history, reenacting old patterns of behavior endlessly and expecting different results. I look to be rescued by some savior because I am unable to stop my destructive course. I am torn inside, divided, at war within myself: I smoke and fight to quit; I eat too much and diet obsessively or am torn by guilt; I hoard and collect; I am addicted to one thousand things and cannot stop; and I fight within against what is happening. The spiritual master Arnaud Desjardins has taught that the unmet needs of the infant and child become the desires of the adult: war all the time.

How may a person use her personal history to aid her transformation?

The struggle to understand this question decides a person's direction, her fate, and her ultimate destiny. What is given in this book is not an answer to this question—because each person must arrive at her own answer to this if she is to grow in understanding—but what is given here is this: the means to struggle with this question and to observe what arises. That is all one can ever do for another, if one is honest.

Each of us lives in a prison of our own devising, the walls of which are constructed from our own personal history. The neuropsychologist Paul Brooke states, as a result of his studies, "The extended self, which is what we think of as our self, is essentially a story. It's the story of what has happened to this body over time" (126).We do not see this. We believe ourselves free to choose, and act from this belief as if we were already free.

The first step in one's transformation is seeing honestly that I am enslaved by unconscious forces over which I have no control—that I am helpless before my addictions and driven by my personal history. The shock of seeing this honestly leads me in a new direction with my life, if I can take in—integrate—this shock so that when I forget, I may remember again. Then it becomes the soil in which the real seed of transformation may be planted.

Real help is always and everywhere available to us, but we cannot utilize it because we are not in "the place" where it is available. Instead, we live in the self-made prison of our personal history and cannot see over its walls. Real help, from the guru or God, exists always and only in the present. The present is the source of all help and of all transformation.

Can you intuit the problem then, when I live always and only in my personal history? My personal history thinks for me, speaks for me, and acts for me. Thus I am cut off from my own Being and from the help which exists in the present, which would aid the growth and maturity of the Being. And what is more, I do not want such help, though I may protest that I do. The mind is a status-quo machine.

Master Osho teaches:

> *Ordinarily, we are walking bundles of solutions to prob-*
> *lems that no longer exist. Everybody is so. You are carrying*
> *thousands of solutions for problems which are no more exis-*
> *tent—and you call it knowledge. It is hindering your capac-*
> *ity to know. It is not knowledge.*
>
> *Drop all the solutions that you are carrying. Drop all*
> *the answers that you are carrying. Just remain silent. And*
> *whenever a question arises, out of that silence you will hear*
> *the answer . . . it will not come from you, it will not come*
> *from scriptures, it will not come from anywhere—it will*
> *come from nowhere and it will come from nobody. It will*
> *come from your innermost nothingness.*
>
> Osho Rajneesh, *Take It Easy,* 33.

The mind acts autonomously, without regard for the effects of its decisions on the body of which it is a part. It acts as if it were a separate entity. This fundamental separation within the self is reflected in all of my relationships, in which there is constant separation rather than unity. If I am out of relationship with the body which I inhabit, and I am deeply identified with the mind such that I believe "I am that," then I cannot enter into a healthy and mature relationship with any other human being or with the Earth.

The Many i's

Separation is not relationship. When the mind says "I" it speaks of itself only, and not the body which it inhabits, or of the Being which inhabits the body for a brief human moment. And this "i" which speaks in the mind is not always and in everything the same "i" but is first one "i" and then another, each using the same

name, "i", and each having its own distinct agenda, each struggling for supremacy and temporary control of the body to enact
that agenda.

It is the same with emotion, each emotion calling itself "i".
One "i" will gain momentary control, will enact its agenda making promises which I am unable or unwilling to keep, performing
actions for which I must pay, perhaps for the rest of my life with
deep regret for a momentary act. The prisons and graveyards are
full of such haunted beings who are paying for the rash acts of an
"i" in them which seized control of the mechanism and enacted
its agenda, only to be replaced the next moment by another, different "i" with a completely different agenda, perhaps one dia-
metrically opposed to the other: "What was I thinking!?"

Self remembering places me in a position in the body from
which it is possible to observe this phenomenon of "multiple 'i's'"
within me, and to do so more or less objectively, without identification. But this happens slowly over time, as I patiently build a
body of conscious impressions of myself as a mechanical being,
helpless to resist the power of identification with these "i's".

The problem is that I am deeply identified with many of these
"i's", and I want the goods they are pimping, no matter the cost to
me personally, or to those I love and who love me. That is where
real work begins and real suffering arises. That is where most people leave the Work. They prefer the suffering brought on by those
"i's" over the suffering brought on by careful, non-judgmental
observation of them. It takes a long, long time before I finally see
and feel the truth of this inner state of mine; before that, and for a
long time, it is just a theory which I do not, cannot, believe about
myself. Instead, I believe myself always and in everything to be a
single "i" within, and when I say "i" it is with the belief that I am
always the same inside.

In fact, this so-called "i" which is used constantly, which thinks for me, speaks in my name, and acts for me, is a machine, a binary computer, programmed from childhood and even before birth, in my case, by fear. It is a liar, unable to be truthful because it is able to see only what it has been programmed to see, its own contents, not *what is, as it is*. It is never the same for long, but constantly changes both agendas and behavior. I am not the same in church as I am in the backroom of the tavern, not the same in the bedroom as in the boardroom, not the same with mother as I am with the woman behind the counter. Therefore, "i" cannot be trusted. In me there is a fundamental division. There is the mind, and there is the body which houses it. And they operate with different energies, in different modes, and at different speeds.

Correcting the Division

In order to correct this separation and division, which is from fear, conscious action is required of the Being within. That Being is Presence and Attention. The mind can only operate with its thought if it is able to win the interest and support of Attention. When Attention is not identified with the thought, no thought can long endure. The fact is that I cannot observe any thought for very long. The reason is simple. One of two things will occur when I try to observe a thought: 1) I will identify with the thought—at which point all observation ceases and it will capture Attention, and I will become unconscious, at the mercy of that "i's" agenda unless and until I once again remember myself; or 2) when the thought arises, I will not engage it, moving neither toward nor away from it—both of which are the action of identification—and without the agreement, the identification, the fascination of Attention, the thought has no power of its own to continue, so it will subside. The energy which it represents will be transformed in me into a finer energy. Herein lies the secret to inner freedom from the slavery of identification. *Will of Attention** lies in the ability to consciously hold Attention in its center and not move into identification with the thought or emotion. This is what it means to work.

Placement of Attention Is Destiny

Again, placement of Attention is destiny. I am Presence and Attention housed momentarily in a *human biological instrument.** One becomes what Attention rests on. Conscious placement of Attention in the body, joining it with bodily sensation, intentionally moving it out of the head-brain and down into the body where its center of gravity is located, is the key to inner freedom from the law of identification. It is this conscious movement which joins once again the mind with the body via sensation, and heals the separation from which all of us suffer. This is first-stage self remembering on a fundamental, primary level, this conscious placement of Attention in the body.

Now one is present and awake, present in the body and in the moment: *I Am.** One cannot make this move unless one is awake. It is a conscious move. Only then may self observation take place. Otherwise it is all in the mind, a self divided, and is pathological, illusory, dreaming, a lie.

The human species suffers, and it suffers from identification with the lies of the mind and its supporting emotions. The master Arnaud Desjardins has taught us, "Never believe thoughts associated with emotions." This teaching alone can bring about an inner "shift in context" and change my life, *if* I understand it from my own experience and observation, *if* I have verified its truth for myself.

We live in the age of terror because the mind is based on terror, the "terror of the situation" (to use Gurdjieff's term, as discussed in Chapter 2), separated from its mother (consciousness) and from its matrix in the body. Therefore, it sees fear everywhere it looks, and when it doesn't, it imagines the terror around the next corner, behind that tree, or in the shadows where it cannot see.

Because the mind is separated from its matrix—which is the body—the body suffers as well. It suffers from the disease of the fear-based mind and the decisions it makes which harm the body. It suffers even more because when there is no conscious control from an awakened Being within, the body is left all alone and therefore must operate unconsciously, on automatic pilot, from stored habit, mechanically. The result is a great loneliness. The body longs for a relationship with the silent Being within, and the Being itself, separated from its matrix and out of relationship with it, also suffers from a great loneliness of Being. Therefore, I lead a life of suffering, loneliness and fear. This is the human condition.

The Wish to Die . . . and the Healing

The result of such circumstances is the unconscious wish to die. Thus, the species is on a death trip. When a Being is subjected to such constant loneliness of spirit and is without the understanding to heal it, of course it wishes to die. Our relationships die, our spirit dies, and our bodies die. But what is worse, *we* die before the body dies. We are a race of phantoms, walking dead, with the life gone from our eyes, no life in our faces, no love in our hearts. We are a brokenhearted race of lonely Beings wasting the planet which is our Mother, and wasting away within.

The means to heal ourselves is given to us at birth. We are able to remember ourselves and to observe ourselves. They go together, are one practice. First I remember myself: "I am here now, in this body, in this place." That is a part of first-stage self remembering. I remember who I am: "I am Attention," and so I can consciously move my center of gravity downward, out of the mind, and into relationship with the body which I occupy. This move creates a space within, which Attention may occupy.

However, I see that I do not respect this space; I do not value it enough. Therefore, I do not struggle often to maintain it or to remain there for long before I succumb to the siren's call of thought. This space, this center of gravity, is empowered by respect born of suffering and remorse.

So right now, if you wish, try something for yourself: STOP!

With the book open just here, set it down and bring your Attention down into the body. From the top of the head, try to visualize yourself sitting where you are: your posture, position, and location in the space. Sense your feet on the floor, your body's contact with the chair, your breath moving in and out, the sensations of the body both inside and outside (the temperature of the room, the sounds in the street, smells, like that).

This kind of inner STOP! may be done at any time during the day, just to reorient oneself, to get out of the dominant mind momentarily and reestablish one's relationship with the body and with the Presence within. This is the beginning of first-stage self remembering.

This work to remember myself and observe myself is not a military exercise, even if my tone sometimes sounds that way. It is a gentle, kindly, and helpful practice of right relationship, beginning with myself. It is a healing modality which begins to gently work with my brokenheartedness, my own unique wounding. The means to heal myself is given to me at birth: "Physician, heal thyself," Jesus said. It is the first step in non-judgmental love, this kindly returning to my matrix within. The return to the matrix, which is not in the mind, is such a relief in so many ways. If you wish, you may seek this relief over and over, as soon as you realize your tension, your lack of relationship, and your absence from the present, the *now* of the body.

Self observation is a self-correcting mechanism. It is the means by which one may heal a broken heart—or it reveals a heart so badly broken that only God may heal it, and slowly, slowly it reveals how and where to find God. It is the gift of grace of a merciful Creator. *The destination is the present—it must be constantly renewed with every breath or the connection is lost.*

> *A neurotic is a person who worries about things that didn't happen in the past, instead of worrying about things that won't happen in the future, like normal people.*
> —Henny Youngman

An Economy Based On Theft

No nation can survive the moral burden
of an economy based on theft. We stole the land
from the Indians for which there is no pardon,
and we stole the freedom of the Africans, sinned

against the human heart in order to grow rich
and now we rob the Earth, steal from our own
grandchildren so we are bankrupt, without a match
to light a meager fire to heat our barren room,

or water to ease our thirst upon our cross.
Of all our sins, stealing from the Earth is worst
because it hardens the heart and makes us gross,
unfeeling, spoiled things whose future is cursed.

It is no secret what becomes of those who thieve:
they're hanged and their children grieve.

Red Hawk

CHAPTER 4

Kaya Sadhana:
Making Friends With the Devil

Enlightenment is the ultimate flowering of consciousness. It can happen only when you are rooted in the body, but it cannot happen only with the body. You have to move inwards, you have to transcend the body too. Your roots should be in the body and your wings should be in the soul.

—Osho. *The Dhammapada,* 141.

All spiritual experiences are sensations in the body. They are simply a graded series of sensations . . . what cannot be ignored are the various categories of impressions (samskaras), the shocks coming from outside which are constantly hitting us. We live on these impressions as on the air we breathe and the food we absorb. We must learn to recognize these impressions . . . What is a true spiritual discipline? It is a known rhythm of the harmonized body. All is there. Nothing could be more material than to use the body for acquiring a right sensation of God . . . Through spiritual discipline the entire body becomes the receptacle of divine sensation.

—Sri Anirvan. 5-6.

Kaya sadhana means sadhana in the body and is particularly associated with the Baul path of sadhana. The Bauls are a Bengali sect of wandering minstrels and beggars for whom music, dance and begging are a way of life. My own guru, Mister Lee, instructed us in the Baul spiritual path—as well as in the Fourth Way and Zen Buddhism. It is crucial to the development of consciousness of the whole—not just one center alone—that one brings the practice into the body, below the neck. For the practice of self observation to achieve its function of transformation by freeing one of identification with the egoic structure, especially the intellectual-emotional complex, self observation must take place from a location in the body, not from the mind. One cannot observe the mind with the mind; that is the trap into which so many practitioners, including myself, fall. In order to properly observe the function of mind, Attention must be placed in a bodily position outside of the mind. In the most ordinary terms of logic and common sense, this makes sense.

Kaya sadhana means that the experiences in the process of seeing identification with the egoic structure must take place in the body. The bodily location I have identified for myself as ideal for objective observation is the abdominal region around the solar plexus/heart center . . . that area. When self observation takes place only in the mind and not in the body, then I am thinking about observing and not observing; I imagine I am working and I am identified with the thought of working. One must locate for oneself the objective physical position most conducive for objective observation of the intellectual-emotional complex.

Where in the body is that position where Attention is least likely to be captured and consumed by the egoic structure? And where is that position which affords me the most consistent objective look at the intellectual-emotional functions without identification? "Seek and ye shall find," the Gospels counsel. This is one meaning.

In order for self observation to be effective, it must be kept in the body, in sensation, sensing the whole body, that most fundamental first-stage conscious move. As I am now, there is a disconnect between mind and body. It is this disconnect which keeps me identified with, and thus enslaved by, the intellect, with its constant flow of judgment and negative imagination. When disconnected from the body, fear is the result. One remains in a constant state of low-level anxiety which occasionally flares up into high-level drama, all of it imaginary. To observe deeply and without identification, one must engage the help of the body to anchor and ground the observation. Sensation provides the missing link, the necessary connection between mind and body. Sensation is the key to self observation below the neck. It unites intellectual center with the body, specifically with instinctive center, from which sensation arises. Only then does sadhana become kaya sadhana; when it is in the body, then the body can absorb and transform the energy of what arises without Attention being taken in identification. If Attention is located at the abdominal region, then it allows me the possibility of staying with whatever arises and not being taken by identification.

I do not wish to mislead the reader into believing that the solar plexus is the only or even the best location in which to center the Attention. When I speak of the solar plexus area here, you may in fact find a location in the body which is more suitable for your purposes. This is perfectly good and means that you are searching, seeking, and thinking for yourself, not taking anyone else's word for things—including mine. In order to be safe on the spiritual path, one must verify, verify, verify everything for oneself—no matter how great or admired the guru or master is who is speaking of the dharma. (Please see Chapter 10: *The Solar Plexus*, for a fuller explication of why this location may be a suitable beginning point for the search for the bodily center of Attention.)

Further, what I am most interested in is making that connection between mind and body over and over again during my day. Placing Attention on bodily sensation, sensing the body from a position below the neck, makes this connection. At that moment, one ceases leading a disconnected life. One ceases being a brain without a body. The self becomes more than mere idea. Only then can real self observation take place. Only then can real learning take place. Now the mind is engaged in a practical, efficient, and constructive use of its energies, by remembering to make this connection. At this point, it is the Being who makes the conscious placement of Attention, creating the condition in which learning can take place.

Remaining in the Unknown

This is complete first-stage self remembering: erect posture; conscious placement of Attention at the solar plexus region; sensing the breath; sensing the whole body; relaxing the body. Now observe. The body is learning how to learn. It is the awakened position. Please note: Relaxation of the body does not mean flopsy-mopsy slouch. It means a conscious, alert, aware, erect posture with no unnecessary tension. Furthermore, it may also include absence of identification and no inappropriate emotion.

Once I learn this, there is no end to the possibilities for learning. Learning should be infinite. Learning should be from a position of "I don't know," or "beginner's mind" (*shoshin*, a concept from Zen Buddishm). Only in this state is it possible to "create out of nothing" (Werner Erhard). Once the mind says, "I know," learning stops. But when Attention is actively engaged in connecting with the body via sensation below the neck, one is no longer in the known, which is memory, where the past or known is stored. One is in the *now* of the body, which can't be known, only experienced. One can't know what *now* will bring next. One can only experience, and experience again, and again, *now*. Being in the unknown creates a certain inner anxiety from which the mind tries to escape back into the known by attracting the identification of Attention. However, my experience has shown me that from anxiety and from difficult circumstances arise urgency and necessity. Anxiety is a powerful force for movement, whereas remaining in the known of the mind creates a kind of stasis, a lethargic illusion of security, and a laziness which avoids seeing and feeling. Remaining in the unknown gives rise to the necessity of one being ever more vigilant, of being on guard against the attractions and enticements of "myself." From *now*, intuition replaces intellection. This is learning. Once I am in position to learn, what is to stop me?

Identification with what is observed stops the learning process. Identification is Attention captured by an object. Now, instead of a free Attention capable of learning, there is "I am that," which is identification. I, which is Attention, is captured and no longer free to learn. It is no longer in the now of the body. "I," which is Presence and Attention, has lost the connection.

Identification is the disconnection of mind from bodily sensation. Buddha says, "All life is suffering.//All suffering is from desire." Identification, the breaking of the connection between mind and body, is desire. Break identification by reconnecting, and end mechanical suffering momentarily. Identification is always with the known, which is memory or personal history. When I am in the now of the body, then "I" is free of personal history. In the shamanic tradition, this is what is meant by "erasing personal history." Only then is life real. Only then is one able to receive help from our Creator.

However, if I am sincere in my effort to be present, I will slowly come to realize that I cannot remain present, even for a brief period of time. "I" is taken by the force of personality over and over. In fact, I am taken by the life force in me, which wants to manifest as thought or emotion or movement—as "myself," which is a collection of memories, or personal history. I am taken by this force because I *want* to be, because I am afraid not to be—this force of personality is what I take as "myself" and to be anything other than this "myself" is frightening. I cannot bear to be other than this for very long. I have no vessel inside that can contain both the urgency to manifest as personality and the wish to remain present, both together. To hold both at once, the Yes and the No together, creates an inner heat or friction, an intentional suffering, a conscious moment. And then I am gone into identification again. But if I am able to stay conscious enough to observe myself and to remember myself, in the process of being taken by identification—of seeing and feeling the shift in attitude which takes place in me—a powerful impression is created in me. It is the accumulation of such impressions which gives my wish to be present more force. Madame de Salzmann teaches us,

> *In order to make the necessary effort, I must understand that I am imprisoned. I have to see myself being a machine, to know myself as a machine, and to be here while functioning as a machine. My aim is to experience being mechanical and never forget it.*
>
> *The Reality of Being*, 88.

Right here would be a good time to practice another inner STOP! and consider for yourself what has just been conveyed.

A Self Observation Journal

If you wish to pursue this idea of identification, of being "taken" in one's efforts to remain present, in the now of the body, perhaps it would be useful to consider keeping a self observation journal, at least for a time . . . you decide for how long. In this journal, one may note certain impressions, certain inner, observed photographs, and certain material from within: What most easily, readily, and often captures my Attention when I sit or try to remain present? Are there times, say when I am around food [this is one of my own], when it is more difficult, even impossible, to remain present (around mother or father or sister or brother, certain other people perhaps)? These people may become a source of help for you. Rather than getting caught in your judgments, you may see an opening, a possibility, to use their presence to remember yourself, to find your breath and consciously relax your body—like that. You may find it useful to keep this journal next to you when sitting in meditation, so that once you are done, you may write down immediate impressions of what you have just seen. It may be a small spiral notebook that you keep in your pocket or purse, so it is handy and you can refer to it during the day. Then, at night when you are relaxed and not inundated, take stock of your day. Read your notes. Consider what self observation has shown you about your daily habits of mood, attitude, and bodily relationship as well as your relationships with others.

A Shift in Context

This shift in the location of Attention, finding a place below the neck from which to observe, allows for a shift in context. When Attention is located in the abdomen, at the solar plexus region, and focused on bodily sensation, one is not at the effect of personal history, which is housed in the head-brain, in the memory function, and also in the emotions. The two work together symbiotically to form what I call the intellectual-emotional complex. Thus one observes outside of the context of my personal history, not identified with it. This is "beginner's mind." I am operating outside of the field of the known: thus a beginner. The result is that whatever arises in the thinking or emotional centers does not automatically get linked with personal history. I do not identify with it; or when I do, then a real impression is formed which can help me. I begin to see what unconscious forces fascinate and enslave me.

At the solar plexus region, personal history is neutralized and the functions of the biological instrument can be observed more objectively. Beginner's mind means a mind unclouded by personal history, a mind whose main task is focusing Attention below the neck. But one must keep observation in the body; one must keep it in sensation. That is the ground from which to observe. That is the sanctuary. Sanctuary is safe place. Kaya sadhana is the experience of sadhana from the safe place, the place from which non-identification with what arises is possible. Then sadhana becomes an objective experience: one observes without identification. Or, one observes identification, studies it as best one can, and begins to collect those more conscious impressions of the process of identification and their accumulation, which gives force to the wish to be present. Then I bring aim from that higher and finer part of me and I make the connection with that life force which demands identification. There is, in the effort to remain present in the now of the body, this linkage, this connection between the higher and the lower. The aim is to see and feel them together, so they become familiar with one another and not separated: to heal the inner separation.

Chief Feature and Blind Spot

When *I am* is located bodily in sanctuary and focused on sensation, *chief feature**—or what I call the *blind spot**—is neutralized. This is called, in Fourth Way language, "reconciling force." [Note: *I Am* is the name which many traditions, including Christianity, give to the inner Being. In the Bible this is one of the names of God.]

I will get pulled out of sanctuary over and over; this is inevitable. But when this happens, as soon as I remember myself, I begin again, return to sanctuary, sense the body, observe.

Chief feature, or blind spot, is the puppeteer, "devil," the one who pulls the strings and to whose tune I dance. Identification with its hooks is what its life depends upon. Its hooks are mechanical, habitual, repetitious, and limited in number. For my own blind spot—my chief feature of self-hatred—the hooks are old and well known. Chief feature is the "devil." It is fear-based. The devil is fear. Any move out of sanctuary is a move into chief feature, or "dancing with the devil." How could it be otherwise? The chief feature is a mechanical construction, therefore predictable: it always reverts to its default position. Thus God, which is love, and the devil, which is fear, are in constant tension in the body. What reconciles this tension, this ongoing struggle, is Attention located at the abdominal region of the solar plexus (or at that point which you have discovered for yourself) and focused on sensation.

The "devil" or "chief feature" or "blind spot" or "cramp" reminds me of assertion: "Just This" in Mister Lee's teaching, or "accepting what is, as it is, here and now" in Arnaud Desjardin's teaching; enquiry "Who am I?" (Ramana Maharshi), or in Mister Lee's school "Who am I kidding?"; and remembrance (remembering the self, the other, and guru or God). It is the lawful function of the devil to serve; it serves to remind me to make the connection with the body, to reconnect to now. Thus, the devil issues the clarion call to practice. The hooks which chief feature uses are hidden in unnecessary thinking, inappropriate emotion, and unnecessary tension in the body. When one is located as Presence and Attention, below the neck, and linked with sensation, thought becomes easier to observe and not so easy to identify with. One may not be so easily hooked. Why?

Because one sees for oneself, and suffers endlessly from, identification with thought and emotion. I have identified myself, my life, who I am, with chief feature. That is why it is *chief feature*: it defines who I think I am. Its power lies in identification. In order for it to maintain its death grip on Attention, it requires that I constantly identify with it.

But the devil is rigid because it is mechanical; its hooks are trackable, which means observable and then predictable, because they are mechanical, habitual, and repetitious. They operate always in the same way. One can become totally familiar with them and begin to predict their behavior: one can recognize instantly which thought patterns will lead to what result, which emotional patterns will result in what behavior, and which bodily postures and tensions will give rise to what thoughts and emotions. And these hooks troll for Attention the way a fly fisherman trolls his fly across the surface of the water, looking for a bite. The trolling process operates as unnecessary thinking, inappropriate emotion, and unnecessary tension in the body. These functions always lead to the same place: the lair of chief feature, where Attention is consumed. It feeds upon Attention. It demands Attention. It is a small child in its development, fear-based, and thus always demanding Attention in order to feel safe. A small child constantly demands attention because it does not feel safe, so it seeks the gaze of the dominant herd leader in order to be reassured. This is classic mammal behavior. Arnaud Desjardins taught that the unfulfilled needs of the child become the desires of the adult.

I do not want to judge myself harshly when I see that I am unable to sustain Attention in the body. That is a trap of the ego. I dance with God and the devil. I am pulled this way and that. I do not have the strength of will to resist. And yet, when I have seen and felt very clearly this constant tension and movement in me, then I may resist this back and forth a bit because *by resisting it I see and feel it more. I come to know it better, more clearly.*

In resisting the urge to leave the present, one can begin to spot the thought and the emotion before they move from impulse to active thinking and emoting. One can see the pull of identification and how, when, why, one is caught and taken and consumed. But for a long time, I do not know how or when or what to resist, nor do I know myself well enough to see that I want to be taken. Patience, patience. This practice builds patience even in an angry, impatient man like me. One cannot believe, even, that one is taken in identification with various "i's" because one does not believe that one *is* various "i's"—one believes oneself to be always the same "i" and thus is taken over and over by the repetition of "i" all day long, with every thought and emotion. And there is the belief that this "i" is always and in everything the same. Thus, one observes in order to come to know oneself.

However, because chief feature, my own devil, is a mechanical construct composed of the same endless, habitual, repetitious patterns, one can, through careful self observation without identification (which means without judgment), begin to recognize these patterns. This kind of observation is work—not easy. Remember that chief feature may also be called "blind spot" because it hides behind certain "i's," certain thoughts, emotions and postures. In my own case, I have become more and more familiar with the patterns which self-hatred uses to capture Attention. Herein lies the advantage: one can become conscious and act from conscious choice. It cannot. One can choose to be present in the now of the body. One can become familiar with blind spot's limited menu of thought and emotional habits. Once I begin to recognize how I am hooked by these same patterns over and over, suffering takes on a new taste: I see what I am when I identify with chief feature. I see how I am the author of my own suffering. No one else is to blame. I choose to identify because I love the known, which is to the mechanical mind the only security. I know the patterns, therefore I choose to remain enclosed in them, out of fear. I do not trust what I do not know. I trust nothing and no one but the devil. Therefore, I do not trust love, which can never be known, only experienced. Love is God. God is unknown. It can only be experienced in the now, which is its only domain.

I have had to seek out professional help to deal with some of these "i's" with which I have deep identification. Mister Lee counseled us: "You're only human; get the help you need." So I have. It is a trap to believe that our work must be done alone. This is relationship work in order to claim my birthright, which is right relationship with self, others, and our Creator.

From Wish to Aim, via Devil

Still, this new level of suffering, brought on by the consistent practice of self observation/self remembering, gives rise in the feeling center to what is called in the Work "wish." Wish is conscious; it is objective, and it is from feeling. Now, given that I willingly undertake what the Work calls "intentional suffering," self observation, in the body, below the neck, becomes true kaya sadhana. It has the training and focusing of Attention from the intellectual center, the linking with sensation from the instinctive center, and a fervent wish which arises from the suffering in the emotional center. At this point, self observation is a three-centered inner process in which all three centers (intellectual, emotional, moving) are aligned and working harmoniously, not warring against one another and constantly stealing energy from one another.

> *Remembering oneself begins to be more complete as my attention is divided and feeling participates. When I am concerned with both the mind and the body, it is impossible for the feeling not to come in—it cannot remain indifferent. My feeling has to be touched either by the quality of my state or by the lack of accord. The particular energy necessary for self-remembering can only be produced at a moment of strong feeling.*
> —Madame de Salzmann, *The Reality of Being,* 84.

From wish, eventually, aim arises. Aim arises from intellectual center, from self observation with feeling, with wish active and remembered as feeling. A friend of mine reported a personal experience in which he clearly articulates this process of arriving at aim through kaya sadhana, actively engaging the suffering of self observation without identifying with it. Through this process he came to identify his own chief feature. The shock of that seeing went through his central nervous system like a lightning bolt. That is not an exaggerated metaphor, it is a lightning strike to the heart of ego. This resulted in creation of aim around his chief feature: "May I never identify with it and may I never forget it." Put simply: Never identify, never forget. This was his conclusion. The conscious accumulation of impressions helps me not to forget.

However, please note his use of the word "never" here. This is like a red flag being raised; it is a setup for failure. Of course I will forget, over and over again. I will forget to the point of desperation and hopelessness. And the shock from the impressions which show me this state of forgetting in myself is invaluable, because that shock may register deeply in the feelings and provide me with urgency and necessity to practice.

Whenever I say "never" and "always" it is a tipoff to me that the egoic structure is making mischief. It is not that the friend's aim was no good, it is simply an example of making an aim which is too large for present capacities. I don't know if this was true of him at all, but I do know that is true of me. I forget all the time. I identify all the time. Therefore, I start small. I begin by taking small bites which I may digest.

The point at which my own devil becomes my friend is the point at which I recognize the value of chief feature's mechanical and repetitious nature. How can this be? Because the devil has only one function in human existence, as far as I can tell: to help me remember God. Our Creator selected from all of its angelic hosts that angel who was most utterly reliable and powerful enough to bear all of human *negative emotion** without identification and thus ruin. Our Creator sent this angel, known variously as Beelzebub, Satan, Lucifer, or denying force, to Earth to stay steady and stable at its post and to draw the Attention of humanity to itself by providing all that we desire, thereby drawing us into brokenhearted ruin and utter hopelessness, from which our only salvation was surrender to our Creator.

Only our Creator is capable of healing the broken heart which my devil has brought about. Thus the devil is not only the guru's ally, it can, when seen and handled properly, become one's best friend in the Work. What else is so reliable, so utterly consistent, always there through thick and thin? When I have suffered its effects enough, and "enough" is relative (for me, it has been more than thirty years of observation), it gives rise to wish and then to aim. At that point, I wish and long to be alert to its (the devil's) every move, and be poised to act, not react. The difference is significant. To react is to battle against what is observed, and thus empowers the devil. Instead, I am called on to act *for* my aim, which is remembered with the help of the devil.

The devil becomes, then, an inner reminding factor which helps me remember myself: self remembering, and to remember at the same time my aim: observe my devil, struggle with identifying with the devil, and never forget it. Madame Ouspensky has said about aim:

> *If our aim is not formed, we are not in the Work yet. If a man has aim he makes demands on himself—a man in the Work knows what he wants, knows right from wrong and is determined to achieve his aim—hates sleep and desires to remember himself and takes everything relative to that.*
> —quoted in: Jessmin and Dushka Howarth.
> *It's Up to Ourselves*, 430.

When one takes chief feature relative to that, it becomes an ally and advisor, not an enemy or tormentor. This is called a "shift in context."

Gentle Struggle for God

The moment I forget that the devil is real and exists in me, it has my number, in the same old tired, formulaic, habitual ways that it always has had my number. But once it has my number, I'm gone, lost, identified and consumed. Unnecessary thinking, inappropriate emotion, and unnecessary tension in the body are the work of the devil. They are the devil's playground. When Attention is in the body, below the neck, and kaya sadhana is engaged actively and consciously, these hooks of the devil become much more obvious. The moment I see that I am identified with the beginning movement of these hooks, at once—*without hesitation*—I wish to gently and firmly bring Attention back to sanctuary at the solar plexus, or thereabouts. If there is any hesitation indicating interest in the hook being offered, the result is immediate identification, and I am lost. Madame Ouspensky says,

> *Where one's attention is caught, one becomes that thing and*
> *of the level of that thing . . . Collecting attention is bringing*
> *it back and bringing it into a definite place in oneself.*
> —quoted in Howarth, 432.

This is not work *against*—neither against my devil nor against ego. Instead, it is work for God, work to make myself available to the influence of the guru and our Creator. Only when I am "in my place" within can this influence reach me and help me. Otherwise it is lost because *I* am lost and unable to be reached.

This work is gentle, not forced or aggressive. It is gentle, healing work, to restore one to one's rightful place within, to reestablish right relationship both within and without, and to return to matrix, that safe place within. That door is always open, has always been open, but my Attention has for so long been turned away from this open door and looking always and only into my own personal hell, obsessed with shadows on a cave wall, the devil's domain.

Look homeward, angel!

Finally, this shift in context can only take place when I have seen my devil at work 10,000 times, and fallen for its allure 10,000 times, and suffered remorse, shame, and inner agonizing 10,000 times.

Only then will I come to the crossroads where I either sell my soul to the devil or surrender to the Divine Love Force. Then I make aim before our Creator and the guru. Then, when I am taken, which I will be, as quickly as I can, I begin again. Over and over I begin again, each time gently and without violence or judgment returning to my place within and consciously engaging kaya sadhana.

Failure is an inevitable component of such aim. Perhaps I learn more from my failures than from my successes. Failure produces suffering and suffering is sadhana. The conscious, intentional suffering of sadhana produced by self observation transforms the Being. Kaya sadhana doesn't take place in the mind. One must bring it consciously, over and over, to the body. Self observation, in order to do its transformative work, has to be done from a point in the body. Here is the beauty of this: built into the mechanical egoic structure is a STOP! mechanism.

Once aim is linked to chief feature, the chief feature becomes a built-in STOP! device. The moment one detects unnecessary thought or inappropriate emotion within, the STOP! may be triggered, and one has the chance to bring Attention back to its sanctuary below the neck, where an objective look, objective self observation, is possible.

All unnecessary thinking and inappropriate emotion lead to identification with chief feature. They feed it. This inner STOP! short circuits the identification process before it can reach the will, in the central nervous system, and capture Attention, thus feeding chief feature. This is conservation of energy, which means one does not struggle against chief feature but uses it always as powerful help in the struggle for aim. Madame Ouspensky has said,

Making demands on oneself is not a question of activity.
Some machines are made to be active. To make demands on

oneself, try to stop the machine in simple ways, which depends on whether one has energy. It should already be clear that you cannot create energy. Necessary save energy, stop wastage. This is possible only if it is your heart's desire and you know what you want.

—quoted in Howarth, 431.

Wish = heart's desire. Aim = knowing what one wants. Eventually there may arise in me the question, "Which 'I' (out of many)"? So in making aim, one needs to be careful about where in oneself such aim arises, under what circumstances, and question if it is according to one's abilities at present—not that an aim for the future has no value, but one needs to address how practical it is here, now.

My Own Devil

The real beauty of the devil may only be finally revealed after years of patient and steady self observation. For most of my life I have thought of myself as weak, ugly, and cowardly, a dishonest man. But it was intense observation of my own devil, which is self-hatred fueled by fear of abandonment, that drove me to get professional help to go deeper into its nature and the hidden innermost feelings which motivated it. Then its real beauty emerged. I saw finally finally that this part of myself which I hated and feared had tremendous integrity, that it refused to yield to pressure from any source, that its courage was enormous in the face of opposition, and that it was where my real inner strength had been locked away and protected from the predations of a harsh and bullying external childhood reality.

Its beauty was a shock, a great surprise to me. And I began to have a great respect and gratitude for this fortress structure, which at its heart was a brokenhearted infant, created out of necessity in my very earliest time on Earth. This structure had a remarkable animal cunning and a superb survival intelligence. It is my friend and ally and has stood by me through the most intense inner storms. It is loyal and steadfast and able to serve my inner work as a consistent and reliable inner reminding factor. My greatest honor and integrity were hidden where I was least inclined to look. That is my starting point.

Fertilizer for Conscience

Thus, one may begin to look at the devil in another way, from another vantage point, with a different attitude. One can actually begin to see "blind spot" as a source of nutrition—fertilizer to feed and help non-judgmental love to grow.

American Indians planted not by plowing up the soil and disturbing the root systems which held nutrients and water in place, but by use of a planting stick—a long stick with a sharpened point. One person would poke a hole in the soil with this planter, and another, often one's child, would follow with a seed bag. She would place a seed from the bag in the hole made by the planter. A third person, often another child, would follow with a basket with fish in it. She would cut off a piece of fish and place it in the hole with the seed, then cover it. In this way, the fish served to fertilize the seed and allow for strong plant growth. In this same way, blind spot is fertilizer, given to us *within*, very deliberately, in order to fertilize the growth of *conscience*,* which serves non-judgmental love.

In other words, the laws of Newtonian physics apply to this process. The first law of matter, which is the law of energy—matter being energy—states that "energy may be neither created nor destroyed, only transformed." Here I wish to change the word "transformed" to "transferred." That is what happens to the energetic force of my chief feature when I stay in place and do not identify with it. That energy must go somewhere, and when it is not used up in identification, it is transferred to some other force within, which may be called "conscience." It becomes fertilizer to feed something higher within. Conscience feeds upon blind spot. To not react to my blind spot is to take responsibility for my life. It allows me to pick up my own cross and carry it.

Conscience must be fed to grow. In this way, chief feature is a Divine gift which allows the establishment of a direct line of communication with the Divine within. What once was seen as a flaw now becomes something invaluable, something which has real value for growth and maturity. This is a shift in context, a change of attitude in which one becomes responsible for one's inner world, not victimized by it.

So, mind your own business! Chief feature, or blind spot, is not your business. It is composed of personal history, and that personal history does not belong to you. It belongs to the mammal and is the mammal's business. Your business is to not interfere with that energy via identification, but to remain in place and allow the energy, which is blind spot—it is an energetic phenomenon—to pass through the central nervous system without interference.

The blind spot is that place created in me as a little child as a place to hide and protect my love from being stolen or hurt. Thus, all of the energy of my love was stored in the blind spot so "they" couldn't take it from me. This is how I shut down and went into a defensive posture inside, developing a strategy to avoid relationship which I then called and identified as "me-myself." By accepting this energetic phenomenon without judgment, allowing it to have its place in me, the energy of the blind spot is released. It is no longer withheld or shut down or repressed. So it becomes available to the body to process and transform, following the first law of energy.

By not interfering with its energy, stealing it to enact the agenda of chief feature, the blind spot becomes a sacrificial offering to God. A portion of this energy is transferred to Presence via self remembering, and to Attention via self observation, thus feeding the Being and allowing it to grow. At the same time, a portion of this energy is sent upward to feed the Divine. This is real Being-food. So mind your own business! The mammal's personal history is not our business. It is the mammal's business. The body knows what to do with this energy if I do not interfere. The Being has no personal history—it is a present phenomenon only, thus without history of any kind. When I accept and sacrifice, I feed the energy of blind spot to the breath, which then circulates it throughout the central nervous system, and thereby transforms it into finer food capable of feeding the Being and the Divine.

Conclusion

When I intentionally and consciously move this sadhana below the neck, returning to sanctuary at the abdominal or solar plexus area, this is the point at which an inner Stop! may occur.

When I remember, I repeat the name of God: Yogi Ramsuratkumar, or Lord Jesus Christ, or Lord Krishna, like that, or I simply remain in the brief silence within.

What I have observed is that when I become more sensitive to the subtler, finer energy within, most of the time when I remember this holy name—and you must verify this for yourself—there is a subtle energetic reverberation which travels up and down the entire central nervous system and is felt throughout the body. This subtle energetic reverberation from the repetition of the name of God suggests to me that it is one way in which one may consciously build an inner structure, or a "second body," as Arnaud Desjardins suggests. This conscious practice of kaya sadhana allows the human biological instrument to assume its higher function as a "transformational apparatus," as Mister E.J. Gold calls it.

In all such cases as those I am describing here, one must test carefully and patiently, verifying for oneself what is true, not falling for the trap of taking the word of others mechanically, in which case nothing of value can possibly be gained. There is no so-called expert here, only a practitioner like yourself, a beginner who wishes to be free, with the help of the devil. It is too easy for me to sound dogmatic and certain, when what I wish to suggest is delicate and very soft, more of a prayer than a rigid rule, a kind of inner dance and not a martial parade.

I end with this from Madame Ouspensky:

> *Everything depends on whether you really want, or you only think you do. Work is not living in house or coming into special conditions, or reading books, or coming to lectures or listening to readings. None of this leads in direction of Work or aim from system point of view. People are divided in two categories—those who think and those who really want. If one really wants, one does. God gives one free choice. No one forces you to do it…Until one sees oneself as one is, and it may mean going many steps backwards from what one thought one was, one has no starting point.*
>
> —quoted in Howarth, 431.

Repeated efforts over a long period of time will create in me real wish—or what Madame calls "want." A sense of urgency will slowly begin to form, in the feelings. It is this urgency of feeling which gives force to the wish to remain present. Repeated failure, and its attendant intentional suffering, is how will develops. One must have the patient courage to enter deeply into relationship with the whole of oneself, seeing and feeling both weaknesses and strengths without judgment, but with real affection, even gratitude. It is the only way real Attention may grow.

The destination is the present—it must be constantly renewed with every breath or the connection is lost.

I was so self-conscious, when I went to a football game and the players went into a huddle, I thought they were talking about me.

—Jackie Mason

Nothing Left

Nothing interests me anymore.
The days crawl by like
worms after a hard rain and
I can sit here on my screened porch
from dawn until dark, doing nothing
just watching the shadows move
from one tree to the other until
everything is bathed in a pale dark,
like my empty heart.
Sports used to interest me but they have
been completely corrupted by greed
and a brutal disdain for the fans.
The newspaper once held some hope for me
because of the funnies, but no more:
Calvin and his tiger were the last breath
of true madness and common idiocy
left in a waste of the simply stupid.
TV is one crushing bore after another
interspersed with deafening commercials
duller than the worst shows.
I sit here on my screened porch and
all of a sudden here she comes again.
Every day this beautiful woman with
long brown hair nearly to her gorgeous butt
comes walking. Today she has on tight shorts
and her legs are splendidly muscled, the
calves curved and bulging, the thighs
2 tapering pillars of tanned flesh so fine
I can almost feel the hairs with my lips

and then she is gone over the hill.
Where was I? Oh, yes
nothing interests me
anymore.

—Red Hawk, *The Art of Dying,* 105

CHAPTER 5

Shifting the Assemblage Point: The Second Ring of Power

(Self Remembering: First Stage Elaborated)

I need to see that what is lacking is a connection with my body . . . Yet my body could be the greatest support for experiencing my existence. It is on the level of the earth and draws its strength from it. The action of our life is on this level . . . not somewhere up in the air. I have to feel the body on the earth, the ground. I do this by sensation—sensing its weight, its mass, and more important, sensing that there is a force inside, an energy. Through sensation I need to feel a connection with my body so deep it becomes like a communion . . . A conscious man would have a permanent sensation of himself and always know how he was inside. So our first aim is to develop an inner sensation.

—Jeanne de Salzmann, *The Reality of Being*, 63.

At the same time that there is an unconscious urge to die in us, there is an equally great urge to live. The result is a great inner division; a war goes on in me between the Yes and the No. The moment I take a position and choose sides in this war, already I have lost the battle. Now I am identified. I do not remember myself. The secret is to find an inner position which stands between the Yes and the No, between the urge to die and the urge to live, and does not enter the fray on either side—a neutralizing force within.

There is a place within where Attention may rest, a space which is neutral, a place between two opposing forces which reconciles them. I am calling that place the region of the solar plexus. If I place my index finger on the soft spot just below the breast bone, and spread the other three fingers down toward the navel from this point, the area covered is the solar plexus area—between the heart chakra and the navel, the mid-abdomen.

This area is sometimes known as "the second ring of power" [I take this term from Carlos Castaneda's book by that name]. This is what I call "the ring of listening," and locating Attention here brings me into the domain of the unknown. The first ring of power is the mind, and it uses its power of thought and imagination to dominate and control the human biological instrument, and therefore the life of the Being housed within it. In this first ring is found one "assemblage point," the place where one version of reality is assembled and disseminated into the world. This version is fear-based and it is a lie. It is contaminated, colored by my personal history and is a summation of that history, which calls itself "me-myself." It assembles its version of reality according to its preexisting patterns, selecting only that data which supports and validates those patterns. Its only purpose and aim is to preserve, restore, and replicate those patterns, at whatever cost to the organism and the Being within. And since it is fear-based and separated from the body and from life, from love and our Creator, its deepest unconscious wish is to die.

In order to observe the activity of this first ring of power, one must find a location outside of it so there is a chance to not identify with its contents and movements. Real self observation occurs outside of this ring, from the second ring of power, located below the neck, at the solar plexus/heart center/abdomen area. Attention will naturally find its center of gravity eventually. This second ring may be the solar plexus, as I've suggested, or another location, but in any case it needs to be a position outside of the first ring.

The conscious placement of Attention at the solar plexus is first-stage self remembering but is not, in itself, a complete action. It is a beginning of true remembrance. It is the conscious act of freeing the Attention from the slavery of the first ring. It is a movement which cannot happen unconsciously, mechanically. I must remember myself, invoking Presence, in order to accomplish this move. From the region below the neck, one may find an inner sensation; one may sense the whole of the body and in so doing one joins Attention with sensation. The joining of Attention with sensation is the missing link in me, which joins once again the mind with the body. This simple conscious move of self remembering heals the great inner separation. It is a move into a conscious realm, a movement of Attention into a position which is not contaminated by personal history. This struggle to be present in the now of the body is what develops and strengthens both Presence and Attention. *The destination is the present—it must be constantly renewed with every breath or the connection is lost.*

The moment one makes such a conscious move, one drops personal history and enters into the realm of the unknown, that which the mind most fears and will do anything to avoid. All that can be known, all that can be named, including God, love, and eternity, including all the ideas in this book, is found in the first ring of power, the category of the known. All thought is from the known, from the past. In the second ring of power there is no thought, only the vast silence of the unknown, where our Creator and the guru reside.

The second ring of power is the present. Lao Tsu calls this conscious movement of Attention "the journey of a single step." The conscious placement of attention at the solar plexus, or thereabouts, means I am here now, present in the now of the body, in the presence of the great Presence within, which is our Creator or the very Self. This is one of the basic fundamentals of what is meant by self remembering. This conscious movement unites the inner world, links mind and body, harmonizes the Being in alignment with our Creator. It is the journey home, where Attention finds its center of gravity. It is a return to organic innocence (Lee Lozowick) and organic ignorance (Da Free John)—but unlike the innocence of the child, this is a wise innocence (Lee Lozowick). I make the conscious choice to return to innocence, knowing the cost and choosing to pay it in order to be available to love-as-present phenomenon. Wisdom is a present phenomenon only. From this position one may access real wisdom, which does not come from me and cannot be owned or hoarded by any human being, but comes directly from our Creator. Only when one is aligned with the Divine may one access what It knows.

I do not know what the Divine is. It cannot be named. Lao Tsu says, "The Tao which can be named is not the eternal Tao." When I move into the second ring of power I am aligned with a power which cannot be named or known except through direct contact and personal experience. It cannot be spoken about. It never speaks. It is the great silence, the void, nothingness, emptiness, consciousness, and from it, all form, all of creation arises. These are names humans have given It. It has no name. Can you intuit why the mind is terrified to go here, and when one moves into this realm it begins to unscroll all of its patterns and images to call Attention back to the mind, to its ring of power and dominance? It has no control in the second ring. There, it may only serve, not rule. Thought cannot move and unroll if Attention remains in this spot, its home and center of gravity. Without the power of Attention, thought is helpless to move. It may only move on command then, and not of its own volition. This is the realm of non-judgmental love.

Breath Is an Ally

Once Attention moves to the solar plexus region, then one can sense the breath, that great ally, friend of the Being in its struggle to awaken. The breath is always and only a present phenomenon, an objective feedback mechanism. The breath is never anywhere but in the present. To sense the breath is to know that one is awake and present to the Presence within. The breath will never fail. When Attention is caught and taken in identification with the intellectual-emotional complex, as soon as one can find the breath, one can be free and present once again. This is yet another very simple step in first-stage self remembering, and it is a life saver. The breath releases stored inner tension. It helps to relax the body. I am breathed and observed by a *"look from Above."** I allow myself to be seen.

I am held in the breath, comforted by this friend from the moment of birth to the moment when I exit the human form. Thus, I have several certain and objective signs which help me to know when I am awake and in the present, ready to self observe: erect posture; conscious placement of attention at the solar plexus/abdominal region; sensing the breath; sensing the whole body; and relaxing the body. This is the Practice of Presence;

therein lies the whole of the first-stage self remembering, the objective process by which I arrive with certainty in the present. I am awake, present in the now of the body, united, whole, aligned, and able to observe the self. First self remembering, then self observation. One step at a time, first things first, then everything else will follow.

The Masculine and the Feminine

This conscious movement of Attention below the neck and into the body, restoring connection and relationship with the body, is a masculine move, an act of conscious "doing." It is masculine energy which holds Attention in its place here and, in so doing, creates sanctuary or safe place, which allows the inner feminine energy to emerge and receive. Thus the masculine remains in an "active-passivity" holding Attention, and the feminine assumes the "passively-active" role (the terminology derives from Arnaud Desjardins) in order to receive the help from our Creator which is available for transformation in the present. The feminine is receptive energy. Thus the masculine and the feminine are joined with this movement, a perfect marriage within. This is the awakening of the feminine, or the feminization of the inner work.

The step into the second ring of power is a leap into the void. One will need to make this movement over and over, see the results, and compare them with the results which come from mind alone separated from all existence and from its matrix in the body. From accumulation of such impressions, not taking anyone's word for this, one may learn that the void can be trusted. This is where keeping a self observation journal can be so useful because the gradual accumulation of impressions lessens my fear of the unknown. One wishes to be gentle and kind to oneself, not harsh and intimidating.

This path that I speak of, the path of self remembering/self observation, is not a path of faith. I must verify, verify, verify everything for myself on this path. Only then will true faith arise in me. I have seen it in myself. I am a man of little faith, a mustard seed only. And yet, from years of practice of this path, a great faith has arisen in me—a faith in the guru, a faith in our Creator, a faith in the wisdom of the body, a faith in the unknown silence within, a faith in the Work, a faith in the present, here now. This Work has shown me that it is my friend, that it has a vast intelligence far greater than I can comprehend, and that from this void the miraculous arises. The great miracle is that the Miraculous resides within me.

I have a new philosophy. I'm only going to dread one day at a time.

—Charles M. Schulz in "Peanuts"

Shifting the Assemblage Point

A Nagual is a shaman whose energetic configuration
gives Him the power to take responsibility for the fates of those
who make up His company of apprentices. Such a Nagual
is Mister Lee, one whose personal power is such that He is able
to guide the fates of 100 or so apprentices, often from
great distances and with subtle moves and magical passes which
He is an artist of the greatest skill at hiding and
camouflaging under the guise of ordinary activities such as
playing Bridge.

In order to accomplish a very difficult maneuver with me,
shifting my inner center of gravity to save my life, He used the
        Bridge table
as His medium. On 3 separate occasions over a 12 day period
He maneuvered me around the Bridge table so that once I sat
opposite Him as His partner, and twice right next to Him,
        observing
His play of the hands.
On the fourth occasion He placed me with 2 of His most
        accomplished
clowns to lighten my inner mood, which is always overly serious
        and self important.

Once He had prepared my inner world to accommodate the move,
on the 9th day He maneuvered me through His Tavern space and
when I failed to hear His invitation to join Him, in one brief
        sentence
Red Hawk is lost in contemplation,

He shifted my center of gravity from the head to the body, as
    neat and
efficient a magical pass as I have ever seen; He accomplished with
as little show and as few words, with a minimum of effort and
    subtlety,
as difficult a rearrangement of the inner structure as I could
    possibly
imagine, one which I will be years integrating and my body has
    still not

recovered from, but has undergone a fierce and difficult inner
    purging of
accumulated emotional poisons. His final move, to fix the
    assemblage point
in its new position, was on the 12th day, very early in the
    morning before Sunrise;
it was so elegant and effective in its simplicity that I will never
    forget it:
I stood before Him in bare feet, seeing Him off on his 4 month
    trip to France.
As He passed me I said, God Bless you Sir, and in one quick
    move He
flashed His gaze into my eyes and briefly touched my arm with
    His hand,
relocating my center of gravity from head to heart.
This is why Mister Lee

is the Master of our company,
responsible for the fates of His party of apprentices.
He wastes no motion,

makes only the necessary effort,
no more nor less,
gets the job done
without pretense or show, invisibly,
impersonally, objectively, cleverly disguised
so as not to call undue attention to Himself.

He is the Unknown Force in the known habitat,
the Magician who pulled this rabbit out of the Devil's hat.

Red Hawk, *Mother Guru,* 88

CHAPTER 6

The Sorrow of Judgment

That is all we need to do: Give full, permissive, loving attention to absolutely anything that we see in our minds, in our bodies, in our environment, in other people . . .

—Thaddeus Golas, 18.

We live in the vale of sorrows, bathed in tears and drowning in sorrows, seeking constantly for a way out. We live in the world of judgment, which is from the mind. All judgment—*all* judgment—is a strategy to avoid relationship. The mind, as we are using that term here—as the memory unit, the "formatory apparatus"—is a binary computer, which is how it is constructed by the human environment in which it is placed. That means it breaks everything, everything, down into two parts. It cannot do otherwise. It is formulated to be a binary machine. Thus, by its very nature, it breaks all phenomena down into two parts. It separates and divides. Fear separates and divides. Have you observed the action of fear? Have you seen this for yourself? If not, stop here and do not return until you have verified for yourself the truth of this observation, not just once but over and over again. Fear separates and divides. Love unites.

Therefore, the very action of the unconscious mind, without conscious volition and control, is fear. The structure of the thinking mind is fear. Thus the directive: observe unnecessary thinking (see *Self Observation, The Awakening of Conscience*, pp. 32-33; or Chapter 13 in this book). Unless the mind is operated by conscious volition from the Being in order to give forth necessary information—to remember, to solve a technical problem in the present, or to communicate (these are its appropriate and necessary functions)—its every mechanical movement is fear. All mechanical, unconscious movement of the mind, all unnecessary thinking, is fear. Thus, all judgment is fear. Judgment comes from the mind. It is fear-based and a strategy to avoid relationship.

Do you have judgments about your body? Such judgments are a strategy to avoid relationship with the body. The result is that I am out of relationship with my own body. Thus the body operates from the deep sorrow of separation grief and separation anxiety (see Chapter 3). Because mind has lost touch, is out of relationship, with its matrix, it goes crazy from terror and sorrow. Continuous terror and sorrow will drive any living creature insane. When the body is not under the conscious control of the Being within (that's you), it operates on autopilot, which means from its stored memory, the accumulated memory of your personal history.

This personal history is stored in the mind and the body both. It is the past. It is never in touch with the present, with reality. The mind works by association. *This information I just received is "like" all this other data which I like, or it is not "like" and therefore I don't like, so . . . into the other warehouse.* To perform this activity, the mind is constantly judging everything in order to catalog and store incoming information. It judges everything, including myself and itself. It is a fear factory, programmed by madmen (says Mister Gurdjieff), and its every mechanical movement is a judgment and is fear-based. It is a strategy to avoid relationship. It has no clue how to operate in relationship because it operates exclusively from fear, and fear separates and divides, so relationship is impossible. Mind's own movement as thought is a strategy to avoid relationship with the present, with reality, which is the only place where non-judgmental love resides. Nowhere else, only here now, in what is, as it is (Arnaud Desjardins) without judgment. *The destination is the present—it must be constantly renewed with every breath or the connection is lost.*

Recognizing Love

Real love, non-judgmental love, never judges. It does not condemn, it does not criticize, it is not punitive, it does not punish, it does no harm. It unites, rather than separates and divides; it embraces, it welcomes, it protects, it nurtures. That's how I recognize love. The body knows it instantly. The mind fears and rejects it, of course, because it cannot know or control love. How can I control God? God/guru/present is non-judgmental love. The effort to control love, which the mind constantly strives to do in relationship, is doomed to sorrow and is inconceivable—like the ant with an erection, floating down the river on a twig, hollering, "Raise the drawbridge!"

But how do I know when I am present and awake, conscious, and therefore in the presence of that Presence within? How can I be certain that I am not kidding myself, lying to myself, dreaming, in illusion and imagination, but really, objectively, actually present to the now of the body? The answer is simple and easily verified. The placement of attention at the solar plexus region only takes place consciously. Sensing the breath—which is a present phenomenon only, never not present—is a second objective signal that one is awake. Linking Attention with sensation and sensing the whole of the body—which is always and only in the present and nowhere else—is a certain, objective verification that one is awake and in the present. Relaxing the body is a conscious act. Erect posture, conscious placement of Attention, sensing the breath, sensing the whole body, relaxing the body—these are the objective feedback mechanisms revealing that one is in the present, conscious and awake. This is first-stage self remembering: the Practice of Presence. One of the higher functions of the body is to act as an objective feedback mechanism to orient the Being in the present.

The struggle to be present develops Attention (Madame de Salzmann). The Being—which is what I am—is Presence and Attention. Attention is a point in a field. The field is consciousness, in which all phenomena arise. Consciousness is God. The disciple John reports that his Master Jesus taught, "God is love." This appears to me to be true, according to my own self observation. Thus, consciousness, the field in which all phenomena arise, is love. That love is non-judgmental. To be present in the now of the body is to place oneself in service to, and at the mercy of, this love. It is to become consciously vulnerable. It is the invitation of the feminine to receive love. It is the conscious decision to surrender to love and move Attention out of hell, where it has resided from the moment as a small child that one decided to surrender one's heart to the prevailing insanity and violence of human society.

The mind fears the present because when I am present I am vulnerable, at the mercy of a higher force over which the mind has no control. It is terrified of vulnerability. It cannot surrender. Surrender is not a function of the mind, but of the Being alone, placing itself in the position *to be surrendered.* Thus, there is a continual expansion and contraction of Attention, expanding to become vast, to include all, then contracting in fear into myself again, becoming small.

"Me-myself" is not an entity or a being. What I call "me-myself" is in fact an action. It is a recoil from relationship, from the present. It is a strategic movement to avoid relationship. "Me-myself" is fear in action. This expansion and contraction is a lawful dance of consciousness. Jon Kabat-Zinn, in his book *Coming to Our Senses*, says,

> *Both modern biology . . . and Buddhism would say that . . . you will not find a permanent, independent, enduring self, whether you look for it in "your" body . . . in "your" emotions, "your" beliefs, "your" thoughts, "your" relationships, or any-place else. And the reason you will not be able to locate any-where a permanent, isolated, self-existing self that is "you" is that it is a mirage, a holographic emergence, a phantom, a product of the habit-bound, emotionally turbulent, thinking mind. It is being constructed and deconstructed continually, moment by moment. It is continually subject to change, and therefore not permanent or enduring or real . . . (43)*

An Essential Distinction

The conscious placement of Attention in the present is a surrender of all judgment, but it is not a surrender of conscious volition or discrimination. Therefore, an important and objective distinction must be made between judgment and conscious discrimination. Herein lies a good example of the careful use of language. Mister Gurdjieff has said, "For an exact study, an exact language is needed." (*Views from the Real* World, 60.)

All judgment is a lie. It is fear-based and arises from my personal history, stored as memory in the head-brain's memory function, the formatory apparatus, the thinker. The thinker and the thought are the same. The thinker is my personal history and it is fear-based. Judgment is always and only selfish, despite its insistence otherwise—it is a liar. Judgment always and only separates and divides, because it is fear-based and cannot be otherwise. All judgment is a strategy to avoid relationship. Therefore it feeds separation grief and separation anxiety (see Chapter 3). All judgment is from the past and is a reflection of my personal history.

Discrimination, on the other hand, is an objective assessment of the present situation based on objective observation—not colored by my personal history and its attendant neurotic obsessions and fears. It is a present phenomenon only. It does not arise from thought, and therefore has no words. It is a feeling arising in the gut, a "gut feeling" that something here is off the mark, out of alignment with love. Thus, the natural and sane inclination is to either take immediate steps to correct the situation so that it is aligned once more with love, or to move the body away from the situation unless and until it is resolved by a realignment. One does this when one senses danger. Otherwise, one acts sensibly and reasonably, with appropriate behavior to correct the situation and move it back into alignment. One senses intuitively what is needed and wanted in any given moment, because one is aligned with the now of the body and is "present to the Presence within" (Mister E.J. Gold). This is discrimination.

There is absolutely no need to judge the other or the other's behavior. That is inefficient use of available energy, wasted in fear and therefore creating unnecessary tension in the body which burns up available energy rapidly, energy which could be more efficiently utilized in self observation and correcting the situation at hand. Otherwise, one enters into hysteria, panic, self-defense, and selfishness, avoiding relationship.

Discrimination always *includes* the other, considers the other, considers objectively what course of action is necessary to deal with the situation, and behaves appropriately. Discrimination is an inner sensation and intuition on how to restore relationship, not avoid it. It therefore acts always in the interest of love and not selfishly. Judgment, of course, is the opposite. Discrimination arises out of a present Attention, organically aligned with the present; judgment arises out of an identification with past phenomena, is always about me, and is therefore always selfish.

A BRIEF REMINDER TO THE READER: The structure of this book is "spiral" in nature, thus there is repetition (see the end of Chapter 1), but such repetition adds both new context and new meaning to the ideas. So repetition is useful and necessary here.

Now seems like a good time to begin to study your own judgments about both self and others. Again, keeping some notes in a journal could be useful here—a help for one to remember what one has observed. Be gentle with yourself. See how harsh judgments distort your relationship with yourself, your body, others, and our Creator.

If you ain't crazy, there's something wrong with you.
—Willie Nelson

The Idea of Crocodiles

I have spent a good portion of my adult life
observing the connection between
thought and suffering,
between the mind's ability to imagine

and hold onto an idea in memory,
and the inherent fear which drives that process.
For example, we are in Lake Village on a bayou,
a body of water left by the Arkansas River

as it meandered toward the Mississippi then
changed its mind and took another route but
left behind this idea of a river, the memory of it.
We are preparing to swim in it when the old Black man

fishing near us says, They's crocs in there.
How do you know, I quiz him?
Seen one once, he replies and that
Is that. We

do not go in. I don't ask him how long ago
he saw one, it would not matter if it was 50 years,
and only one, and it long dead, because
the imagination has got hold of it and

now the crocodiles exist and
we are afraid of them.

Red Hawk

CHAPTER 7

The Seduction of Change

The moment you start seeing your faults they start dropping like dry leaves. Then nothing else has to be done; to see them is enough. Just to be aware of your faults is all that is needed. In that awareness they start disappearing, they evaporate . . . Unconsciousness is a must to go on committing the same errors. Even if you try to change you will commit the same error in some other form . . . you will exchange, you will substitute, but you cannot drop it because deep down you don't see that it is a fault . . . the moment one sees one's faults, a radical change sets in . . . the deeper you go the more consciousness is released.

—Osho, *The Dhammapada*, 76-77.

Radical change. "Try it, you'll like it!" But remember, as my friend Werner Erhard says, "There is no breakthrough without breakdown." You cannot, I repeat, cannot change, not even at all, let alone radically, from where you are. Where are you? . . . You are identified with a psychological script that is the result of conclusions drawn by a small child . . . not only physically but emotionally and mentally, and should be no more. You are a mechanical being, chronically habitual and dynamically committed to suffering, illusion, confusion, ignorance, and mightily resistant to every kind of change whatsoever except the horizontal shifts that are a function of that psychological script . . .

> *So you have found the path, possibly me as your guide; you . . . have deeply committed to it and sacrificed for it, and here you are, unable to change as you are. What to do, what to do? You must prepare yourself for radical change by developing, cultivating, a field of softness, a willingness to consider your abject spiritual poverty and the lies you have labored under all your adult life . . . and an unshakable confidence—call it Faith, Trust, Love, or gratitude, even call it Obedience, Devotion or dedication—an unshakeable confidence in your guide.*
> —Lee Lozowick, quoted in *Tawagoto* 24:1, 6-7.

The twentieth-century German physicist Werner Heisenberg ought to be the patron saint of those on the path of self observation. It was he who realized, in what must have been a radical act of intuitive insight, what became known as Heisenberg's Uncertainty Principle: the presence of an observer changes the process being observed. This law changed the way we viewed modern physics, but it is also a law of metaphysics. Osho is restating the law in metaphysical terms in the quote on page 87.

Self remembering sets the stage for self observation to take place. But Heisenberg makes a startling discovery: the observer and what is observed are not separate. There is only one thing happening and it has two components. Observer and observed are one. That is why the presence of an observer can change the process being observed. Only the mind makes a division and sees them as two separate things.

However, when viewed from "the second ring of power" (see Chapter 5)—that is, when Attention is placed consciously at the heart/solar plexus or a spot like that below the neck—something brand new becomes possible. The whole process of self observation can become impartial, objective, impersonal—also known as "witness consciousness." Osho indicates such an inner shift in context in his discourse above. Witness consciousness unites observer and observed, the point (Attention) merging into the field (consciousness), able to view both dispassionately, without judgment or the desire to change anything. Everything settles itself, without trying to change things inside. But this inner shift does not happen at once, or for a very long time. It is the maturation of the practice of self observation done with diligence and perseverance, slowly and patiently, which brings one eventually to the radical, intuitive realization that the observer and the observed are the same thing.

But the first shift in context occurs when I consciously move Attention out of the mind and into the body. In fact, the very presence of an observer within is radical change. "If I see it, I don't have to be it" (Jan Cox, Fourth Way teacher). Whatever I am able to see is not me. Being is the field in which all phenomena arise, and is the observer which sees and experiences the phenomena as well. Habitual, mechanical, unconscious behavior goes on and on, from birth to death, because I do not have the eyes to see within. I am not aware of those inner forces which drive the human biological instrument in the absence of a developed Attention or consciousness. The body and the mind in this unconscious state are separate, thus the body is left to its own devices, alone without a conscious volition which chooses and decides. The mind replays its habitual patterns, and the body either obeys or goes to war. It is the same on the world stage: war after war, violence of every kind enacted upon the Earth, women, children, and man versus man.

The only change necessary in human life is self remembering/ self observation; it is a self-correcting mechanism. The observation of the inner phenomena is revolution, not against anything, but for more consciousness, more Presence. If the struggle is against anything, that is identification, and self observation ceases at that moment. The struggle to be present, in the body, and to remember myself, develops both Presence and Attention, creates for them an inner structure. This is a struggle *for* more consciousness. *The destination is the present—it must be constantly renewed with every breath or the connection is lost.*

The Trap of Change

The desire to change what is observed is a trap in the practice of self observation. If judgment is the first trap, then the desire to change what is observed is the second trap brought about by judgment, and many fall for it. Both come from identification with what is observed. If I believe that the observer and the observed are separate entities, then I identify with the observer, and I judge what is observed. Then I begin a struggle against what has been judged as "wrong" or "bad" and now there is a split, a division, a war within. This is insanity.

One begins to observe with what is called "observing i"—a single "i" or a group of "i's" which have heard and understood the need for work on self and wish to engage in the practice. Inevitably, such observation leads to constant identification and results in suffering, because such "i's" begin slowly to see that they are helpless. This leads to an ever-deepening series of shocks, which gradually serve the function of awakening the unconscious

Being within. Now a new force, from a different level, has entered the field of observation. The awakening of the Being provides new possibilities.

Our entire society is built upon trying to change. The whole self-help movement, a billion dollar industry, is about tempting people with the promise of change. The diet industry, the whole of advertising, are all built around this desire in me to change my life. The inevitable result can only be sorrow and an ever-deepening guilt and its accompanying self-hatred. All war is from this mistaken belief that I can be the instrument of change.

What prevents real, substantive change from occurring within is interference with the process being observed. I identify with it and I forget myself; I do not remember. Trying to "do" something about what I observe is interference. It is not minding my own business. It is not my business to change what is in me. I cannot do it, even if I desire to. I don't know anything. I am ignorant, driven by habit and lies, and it is this complex of intellect and emotion which desires to change things. Only chaos and sorrow can result. The fact is that it is the work of our Creator to create change within. My business, my real work, is to place myself in the position of receiving help from Above. This help from Above is always, always available, but I do not know how to access it. Instead, I constantly believe that I can do it by myself—in fact *must* do it by myself. It is a long process of intentional suffering which leads me to the realization that I know nothing and can do nothing about my situation. No matter how hard I try, nothing changes. I am helpless before my habits and my life is out of my control.

This is a revolutionary realization, a "Being-shock," and it leads to the most radical action a human being can take: invitation to surrender. The journey to my knees in surrender is the journey of a lifetime. It is what I do every time I remember myself and consciously place Attention below the neck, perhaps at the area of the heart/solar plexus. I am placing myself in the position to receive help. But I am easily seduced for a long time and almost immediately taken by thought and emotion. I forget myself, I forget my aim, and I am trapped under the law of identification. *I am* no more. I am a robot, mechanical man, a creature of habit.

One has to see and feel this mechanicality many, many times; it is this accumulation of impressions of habitual unconscious behavior which brings force to wish and aim.

Take a moment just now to sit up straight and come back to the body, sense the breath, sense the whole of the body, and relax it. Be easy for a moment. When I use the words "helpless" and "out of control" here, those are relative terms; they do not mean that I cannot exert a certain "will of Attention" (Mister E.J. Gold) and bring myself back into the present, into the now of the body. What is implied by their usage is that real, meaningful, and lasting change is out of my control. See what is possible right now for yourself—not some long-range fight to change anything, but right now, very practically, take stock, see what your present state is. Where is the tension in your body? Where is your Attention? Relax. Be kind. Help yourself to be more present to the help from Above. Where are you right now? Learn to love yourself as you are by placing yourself in the domain where love exists: the present moment. The gentle move to relocate the Attention lower in the body is in fact an act of love, of kindness, and of self-worth. Every time I make this conscious move to awaken is an assertion of self-worth. Dance with it; dance with God. Move gently and with affection into the lawful expansion and contraction of consciousness. Be in that flow, relax into it, let go.

One thing I will learn quickly about myself, if I am at all diligent in self observation, is that I cannot remember myself. How can I observe myself if I cannot remember myself? It is impossible. I imagine that I observe myself, I lie to myself, and I believe in my own lies, as always. But it is all from the mind. I do not remember my body, which is the first-stage self remembering. All I am is a mind, a mere idea, disconnected from its matrix. A divided self, separated from its matrix, is lost and lonely and alone. When that happens, the wish to die arises. With this realization, kindness becomes a real necessity. There is no need for me to judge myself because I see that I cannot remember myself. This seeing is intentional suffering—and it is voluntary. Simply, whenever I remember, I return to love, which is the present moment. I merely have to sit quietly, assume an erect posture, and sense the breath, which is my loyal companion.

The Reminding Factor

In order to remember myself, I need help. I need a reminding factor to remind me to remember myself and what this great Work is. There are many "i's" in me which do not remember this Work at all; they operate in complete unconsciousness, oblivious to the very existence of this inner work on self. When I identify with such an "i" I go into the darkness and am lost completely to myself and the Work. One "i" in me which is like this is the terrified, panicky, infantile and brokenhearted "i" associated with food. It is extremely difficult for me to remember myself around food. That "i"—which was created from earliest infancy in the orphanage and foster homes before my adoption—is feral, fearful, very clever, and crazed. It wants all the food it can cram into its empty loneliness. It is a great ally to my chief feature of shame and self hatred. So when it is done gorging, shame and self hatred follow it as the shadow follows the body. They go together as a bonded pair.

Thus, such an "i" in me may, with long and patient observation, become a great ally for the work. It may be transformed into an inner reminding factor which helps me to remember myself and do this work. This is one struggle in me, not to work against or fight this "i"—a battle I cannot win—but with slow, patient self observation, keeping it steadily in my gaze, seeing and feeling its effect and influence in me, and without judgment (when I can), to bring this "i" into my inner *work circle.** Thus, it can remind me of my aim: to straighten my spine and consciously place Attention at the heart/solar plexus, sense the breath, sense the whole body, and relax the body . . . now observe.

Sometimes I am able to utilize it in this way. Sometimes I eat this "i" and sometimes it eats me. This is what work is. "I's" such as this may serve my work if I am able to bring more consciousness to them. They may actually help me remember myself and my aim.

I have in me several "i's" whose service is to my shame, my self-hatred, my blind spot or chief feature. Some of them I have utilized quite successfully, after long, long struggle and suffering, in the service of inner reminding factors. They help me to remember myself. They help me remember that I have a body. I am in this body, in this place, at this time, here in the now of the body. This is what the work can do for me. I cannot change by myself, but with the help of the inner work on self, if I do my part, which is to remember myself and observe myself without judgment or trying to change what is observed, I can be remembered and our Creator in its mercy will change me, *if change is necessary.* My work is to not interfere with what is observed. When there is judgment, there is interference with the work of our Creator. The next step following judgment is to fight against, to try to change, what I do not like. This is interference with the work of our Creator.

So another, a far more mature level of self remembering, is to remember my place and stay in my place, mind my own business and allow a higher force in me to do its work *on me*. I remember our Creator, who is in me—but this is still far away.

Mind's Supremacy Rests Upon the Three "C's"

Conflict

Perhaps you see the beauty of all that is described here. This practice is a dance, remember—it is the dance which accompanies the birth of self-worth. My work is conscious posture and the conscious placement of Attention, the movement of Attention—of the center of gravity of the self—from the mind to the body, the solar plexus or the heart region; to sense the breath, sense the body, relax the body, observe without judgment. When I do this, our Creator will do the rest. It is a law. But here is the catch: the mind will say this is too easy; there HAS to be more to transformation than this.

The mind maintains its supremacy in the body by creating conflict. Conflict feeds the mind's fear. Simple as that. Conflict feeds fear. So the mind wants to fight. Perhaps you have seen this in yourself. If you have not, then STOP! here and do not return until you have verified this for yourself—not just once, but many times.

And the mind will make up lies and generalizations and judgments about others in order to create such conflicts, in which it thrives and grows stronger. The law is: what gets fed grows stronger; what does not get fed weakens and dies. To verify the nature of mind, it is necessary to cultivate a listening posture: listen to the mind as if you were listening to a CD or radio; take some notes so that you record precisely what you hear. Become a disinterested observer. The desire to change what is observed creates inner conflict. Now there is a self divided, one definition of insanity. One "i" has judged another "i" and now goes to war with it in order to try to change it. The moment one enters such a battle on either side, one is lost. The work is to stand between the Yes and the No and to not interfere. Mind your own business. Find your work, do it with all your heart, let nothing come between you and your work (Buddha). Let God do its work, you do yours. Mind your own business. Dance with your Maker.

Confusion

Another way the mind maintains its supremacy, besides creating conflict, is by creating confusion. My work is simple, not easy; it certainly is not easy to remember myself and observe myself, but it is simple to understand. Now that I know what it is that I wish to work *for*, I have a very clear and simple aim: self remembering—conscious placement of Attention. The mind will take this simple aim and create confusion out of it. It will try to make things complex and difficult. It will throw its most seductive habit patterns up to steal Attention and run these patterns. It will lie. It will attempt to seduce the Attention into identification in any way it can.

The mind is not alive. It is not the enemy. It is a binary computer and, as such, it has only one simple aim, the aim of any computer: to store, protect, and repeat its stored patterns. Period. It does not act in the interest of the Being. It has only one self interest and that is its own memory banks, which it examines and repeats until it dies . . . unless consciousness is allowed to grow and mature. What can do this? Self remembering/self observation. They are the same thing. We are given this single, simple tool that comes with the human biological instrument and is meant to maintain, restore, and repair this miraculous machine.

I am an apprentice mechanic. I have learned to use this tool just a little bit. I have not mastered this tool. I am no master, nor am I a guru or a teacher. But I have faithfully stayed with this single, simple tool of self remembering/self observation, and it has taught me and changed me, radically. I am here to witness this and to speak of this miracle with you. If you have eyes to see and ears to hear, then this tool can go to work for you and you may work with it as well. Dance until your heart catches fire.

Contradiction

A third way the mind maintains its supremacy and steals Attention to do so, besides conflict and confusion, is through contradiction. One "i" constantly is in contradiction with another. I say one thing and do another. One day I make a promise which the next day I have no intention of keeping. Why? Because the "i" that made the promise—to love, honor, cherish, and obey for example—is no longer in control of the instrument but has been replaced by another "i" whose only interest is in chasing and having sex with women. *Love, honor, cherish, and obey? Are you kidding? Look at that fine babe!* Like that . . . that's what I mean. I am a mass of contradictions and I do not see them, nor do I care for them to be called to my Attention by well-meaning acquaintances, like my wife. The mind creates a series of what are called *buffers** whose only function is to keep me blind to my contradictions. Conflict and confusion are just such buffers.

But the most effective buffers are guilt, blame and justification. These are supreme in keeping me from seeing my own actions and how they affect those close to me. These are effective strategies to avoid relationship, beginning with myself. I am not in relationship with myself. And these buffers prevent me from observing myself, therefore not actively engaging in conscious relationship with all of me, including those parts—my underworld or shadow world—which I do not like to see and from which I suffer. I am out of relationship with vast parts, worlds, within me. The desire to change myself serves this same purpose—a strategy to avoid relationship. **"Let it settle itself,"** Buddha said.

What does this mean, this dharma? It means that I do not interfere with what is observed. Period. This is an act of faith. One has to trust that, by following the law, all that needs to be transformed will be given by grace. One may begin, finally, to listen, both to what is within and to what comes from outside, from all kinds of sources and angles, often in the most unexpected ways. One listens and senses the help which arrives. But remember, this is not a path of faith. Such faith only arises by observation of grace in action over a long period of time.

Verify, verify, verify. Accept nothing on the word of another; practice what is taught; observe the results, and faith will be given to you. So I do not speak from some book, or some borrowed knowledge; I have come to faith through observation and personal experience. This "God" which cannot be named has shown itself to me through action. Therefore I have faith. I place my hope in what is permanent, rather than in the fluctuating impermanence of the mind. I place my hope in consciousness, not in thoughts.

This work needs a group. One of the tricks of the mind is to convince me that I may work alone. I need the feedback mechanism which a group provides for my own safety, because I am easily fooled by the mind and its imagination. A group is a mirror to help me see myself. Even in silence, even when listening or preparing to speak, there is an Attention which is larger than the individual when in a work group. Again, one needs to understand that such help will arise lawfully when one engages such practices with honest effort and struggle.

> *When I was a little kid, I had a mood swing set.*
> —Steven Wright

The Simple Life

No cell phone, no caller id, no call-waiting, no
cable, no Tivo, no computer, no Ipod, no
blueberry, no notepad, no laptop, no
riding mower, no leaf blower, no weed eater,
no digital clock, no air conditioner, no new car;
I live in another country, a different century.

I ride my 3-speed bike to work, because
it helps the Earth and eases the body more gracefully
into its dying; it makes the body work hard and
it likes to work, likes to do sweat-labor despite
the avalanche of labor-saving technology whose function
is to drain us of our life force.

I write by hand in a notebook because
I like to see where I've been, follow my tracks back
through the snow, nothing deleted.
I don't want to know who's calling or
who has called. I've lived 65 years and I have
never gotten a phone call that made a difference.

Most people are slaves.
That's the way they like it.
After all the years of heartbreak and disappointment,
of treachery and betrayal, are you so far gone
that you believe the next phone call will be the one
that saves you? When Death comes for you,

(continued with stanza break)

you can't say, Would you mind holding?
I've got a life on the other line.

—Red Hawk, *Self Observation*, 110

CHAPTER 8

Field Attention: The Objective World

(Self Remembering: Second Stage)

The consideration of awareness does not mean to focus on one point only to ignore another. It means that in our training, the development of field awareness, field attention is our aim, where we are open, without blinders, to whatever and wherever the need is—whether it be to the "charity beginning at home" or to pray for the accident victim we pass on the highway . . . We need to see in front of us, behind us, and to the sides of ourselves as well as off to and beyond the horizon. Can you? Yes. Will you? Well, that is not a rhetorical question. Will you?

—Lee Lozowick, *Chasing Your Tail,* 96.

There is relationship everywhere we turn . . . relationship with ourselves in the sense of stalking and observing ourselves, keeping our attention on the entire field around us, rather than fixating obsessively on our personal psychology, expectations and needs. Relationship is truly the source from

which everything—all possibility—flows . . . Letting go and
forgiveness are powerful doorways that take us deeper into
the heart and mystery of relationship, but there is a definite
price to be paid.

—Nachama Greenwald, *Tawagoto,* 24:1, 82.

Nachama pinpoints the danger, the possible pathology, on the path of self remembering/self observation: "fixating obsessively on our personal psychology." That is why self remembering must come before self observation. First I remember myself, I place myself in my physical surroundings, in the now of the body, then I observe. This is the first stage of self remembering. But in the second stage of self remembering, my Attention expands to include more: I position myself in relationship to the outside world and with others. I am not alone; I am in a context, in relationship. Self remembering is about this relationship. It is a further expansion of Attention, aware inward and outward at the same time, I and other equally in my field of Attention, which the Work calls "split Attention." That is, with Attention in the present, in the now of the body, I am aware of myself inside—my reactions to impressions—and at the same time I am aware of the external environment, taking in impressions of the person standing before me. I am aware of the other and I am aware of myself simultaneously. This is what the Work calls "split Attention."

It is only by working to be present that my attention will
develop.

—Jeanne de Salzmann, *The Reality of Being,* 30.

Attention naturally grows and matures with the patient, faithful practice of self remembering/self observation. It is not difficult. It is natural. It is a return to a bodily state which I recognize from my earliest childhood. At some point, the effort to split Attention—or one might even say to *expand* Attention, to include internal and external at once—can lead to a new, more mature level of split Attention known as "field Attention."

This second stage of self remembering begins with the effort to split Attention to include two places, in two directions at once. Ordinarily I am aware on only one level at a time, either all attention inside, or all attention on outside, but never both at once. Madame de Salzmann gives the ratio of 75 percent inside, 25 percent outside. However, with Attention lower down in the body, not fixated in the mind alone, it is possible to observe myself as others see me, from the outside so to say, and at the same time to be conscious and aware of my inner reactions.

A splitting of Attention is possible in which "myself" becomes an object of observation, rather than the usual subjective experience: that is, Attention upon myself in the space which the body occupies—awareness of myself in a physical location—and also Attention upon the object or person or circumstances in front of me. My Attention expands to include more. Thus, Attention expands to include two places at the same time, one internally, one externally. This is second-stage self remembering, the level which moves Attention from *fascination*—that is, Attention aware of only one thing at a time—to what the Work calls "split Attention," or self remembering. Generally, either I am aware of myself when speaking to another, or I am aware of the other when speaking, but never am I aware of myself speaking and, at the same time, aware of the person I am speaking to.

To describe this stage of self remembering one might call it an "expansion of Attention" rather than "split Attention," which may give one a clearer and more easily understood picture of what one is doing with Attention in this stage of self remembering. However, it is also useful to see it as split Attention, in which Attention goes in two directions at once. This splitting of Attention to include two directions at once, which anyone can try if they are informed, is the key to moving into the objective world. From this kind of expanded Attention, one may begin to observe oneself from an entirely new angle; now the possibility of observing without judgment, objectively, arises. However, the moment I react to what is being observed, the moment I take a position in regard to what is observed, I no longer remember myself. I have been taken by identification with my reaction, forgetting myself as impartial, external observer. Now the only possibility is identification with what is observed. I forget myself. Attention is no longer including two places at once: internal and external, subject and object, self and other.

Expansion into Union

This two-pointed split Attention directs awareness on self and other, or on my inner reactions as subject, and the reactions of "other" as object. This is simply sensing the whole of the body, not its separate parts, and also sensing the other's feelings and reactions, so it is accurate to call this an expansion into union. This takes self remembering to a whole new level.

When self remembering is done in this way, it invites relationship, exactly as Nachama suggests above, because I place myself in relationship to my environment. My Attention has a context both internally in its matrix, and externally in my surroundings. As Mister Lee states, this leaves me open, vulnerable but also available, inviting relationship because I am in relationship with the body inside and with others. The classic analogy is to describe this expanded Attention as a double-headed arrow, one point going outward toward the other, another point coming inward to include myself in the context or surroundings, the environment. This is a finer level, a second stage, of self remembering. I think the double-headed arrow analogy is a useful one. This expansion of awareness or Attention to include self and other in relationship is a joining, a union.

When Attention is consciously placed in the region of the heart/solar plexus, I am in my place (first stage). When the Attention is focused both inside and outside at the same time (second stage), then a kind of impersonal observation begins to take hold. I do not take the movement of thought or emotion personally. They are not my business. My business is to stay in place inside, moving neither toward nor away from this relationship with the functions of the body. I do not move into identification. As Lesley Ball, a sangha mate, suggests, I "just hold steady, right there, relaxing into the stillness, feeling without placing [my] attention on the opposing force."

Wide Vision

This split Attention can include what is called "field Attention," which includes another component of second-stage self remembering, besides the awareness of the external environment, or Attention in two directions. Field Attention may also be practiced with what is called "wide vision," or "soft vision," "gazing" or relaxed, non-focused Attention. To practice field Attention in this way, the eyes remain unfocused on any particular object, just taking in the entire periphery, the entire field of which I am a part, the whole of my field of vision, not fixated upon a single point in that field. I see in front and to both sides equally (as Mister Lee suggests), giving no special focus to any object. This type of wide vision, when coupled with conscious Attention at the heart/solar plexus region, brings one into the objective reality, the impersonal life and the objective world in which "I" is no longer the center. In this position, Attention feels itself as part of a much larger field of phenomena which includes self, other, and the higher, all as an energetic continuum. Here, the point merges with the field, which is its matrix. When one is included in this vast field of Attention, of which the individual Attention is merely one point, one begins to sense that "I am" which is larger than the individual self. The Being begins to sense itself as a conscious field of sensitive awareness. At this point, individual Attention is held within consciousness itself, as part of a greater whole in which it serves an essential function as a bridge between the higher and the lower, a reconciling force serving to transform higher energies from above, and lower energies from below, into a middle substance which feeds both my own Attention and then may ascend to feed higher entities.

This field Attention then allows an opening to our Creator as well (third-stage self remembering), in which "I" becomes a still point in a vast field of motion; it recedes into the background, no longer occupying the central, selfish, egoic position. "I" becomes a sacrifice laid at the feet of the Beloved in service and thanksgiving, in adoration and devotion. It is in its place and knows its place.

Now there is no object upon which "I" may fixate. The effort to hold Attention both in the heart/solar plexus area and on the field which is before me, and of which I am a part, may bring about an inner stillness. Thus, with second-stage self remembering, self observation becomes objective and it is much easier to distinguish and observe the slightest movement in the intellectual-emotional complex without becoming identified. This movement into field Attention may be practiced at any time. Use common sense.

The Movement into the Objective World

This field Attention may also be accompanied by what is called "wide-listening" in which one takes in all of the sounds in the field of hearing without differentiating or focusing on individual sounds. Again, this coupled with visual-field Attention moves one into the objective world, from which one may observe oneself dispassionately, impersonally. One is aware of all the sounds in the sonic field, and aware of oneself listening, at the same time (second-stage self remembering). With conscious placement of Attention in the heart/solar plexus region as well as on the peripheral field, the subject-object dichotomy disappears momentarily and one may feel one's nothingness in this state quite distinctly.

This feeling of nothingness is not one which the ego can tolerate and it will seek quickly to recapture Attention with random unnecessary thought or inappropriate emotion, seeking identification in order to utilize Attention for its own ends. If I stay in place, then I can get a very clear look, a "look from Above" to use Work language. This provides what is called "free Attention." Free Attention is Attention which is not captured by identification with unnecessary thought or inappropriate emotion. The kind of split Attention, or expanded Attention being described with field Attention, reveals the emptiness out of which "myself" arises as thought or emotion.

Naturally, when I am with others, I focus on who is in front of me. Otherwise this kind of deep focus bothers people, maybe even frightens them. This suggests the importance of the practice of invisibility; one does not wish to call attention to oneself or one's inner efforts to be more present. But it is possible to unobtrusively focus on the other while at the same time being aware of my inner reactions to impressions—split Attention—without calling attention to myself. That is why work in a group is so vitally important. Group work provides special conditions in which one may try things which, in ordinary life, would call attention to oneself and create mischief. But often, when I am in a crowd, walking through an airport or such, this field Attention provides startling observation of self and others. It is a glimpse into the impersonal life which is quite revealing. I begin to see clearly what distractions I am most interested in. And if I continue to work in this environment, then the moment a distraction (that is, an impression), comes into my view—with me it is so often a woman, or some part of a woman's body which I automatically and mechanically from long habit go to—then at once, without hesitation, I return Attention to the solar plexus, realign, and allow the body to absorb, consume, and digest the impression. I do not look twice, or I am lost. This is the wish to work.

In this state, one finds oneself in relationship with the body and with our Creator, without the usual accompaniment of self-centeredness or self-interest. The self becomes a background—there is self remembering without self-obsession. This might be called "objective self remembering." What remembers in this state? That is a question worth holding without trying to answer mechanically or too quickly. Instead, experiment and find out what your experience reveals. STOP! here and explore.

Time to Practice

I cannot work all the time—I'm not sure anyone can unless one is at a high level of awakening. But for myself, I set certain times of the day and certain activities in which my aim is to work as continuously as I can for a short period of time.

When I sit for meditation in the morning for fifty minutes, I am only making work effort, dancing with God—forgetting and remembering in a kind of pulsation which is occasionally both effortless and a kind of joy, not judging or condemning, merely moving as often and gracefully as I am able into self remembering and self observation.

When I ride my bicycle to work, I set this time to make work efforts, especially wide vision and listening, or field Attention. During the day, when I am able to remember and come to myself momentarily, my effort is to stay present in the now of the body for the length of five breaths (inhale–exhale = 1 breath) and then I let it go. When I am in a crowd, it presents me with rich impressions and opportunities to work. I husband my work energy to utilize it in those times when it is most accessible to me.

One has to be sensible and practical with work effort. I set aims for myself which are practical and do-able, not too extreme or ambitious, but simple and manageable. The fifty minutes of daily sitting practice offers a rich field for work effort. I remember what Madame de Salzmann taught: that the struggle to be present develops Attention. This is my aim. To set aside time every single day in which my only focus is the struggle to be present in the now of the body. Often at night, when I sleep, I will hold the medicine stone, a smooth Buffalo River stone, in my hand with the aim to hold it all night long and not drop it. Thus, I work on building Attention even when asleep.

The best cure for hypochondria is to forget about your own body and get interested in someone else's.
—Goodman Ace

The Body Is Given to Serve the Soul

The Soul grows weary when faced with ease,
but resolute when placed in dire straits.
By nature the body seeks pleasure and hates
pain, but stress strengthens the Soul and frees

it from the body's insatiable desires.
Ennobled by adversity, the Soul grows wise
and trains the body so that it conspires
in its own inevitable demise,

as a wild horse, when broken is defiant,
yet treated with dignity and gently reined
it will become willing, compliant,
a grateful partner trained to serve;
use harsh means and brute force
and you get a broken but unreliable horse.

Red Hawk

CHAPTER 9

Completing the Inner Triad

(Self Remembering: Third Stage)

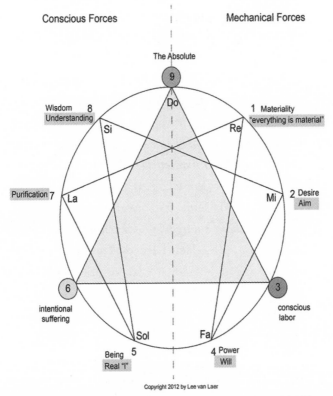

The Enneagram: with terminology from the Gurdjieff Work*

*THE DIAGRAM ON PAGE 111 IS REPRODUCED ON THE INSIDE OF THE BACK COVER FOR EASE IN REFERENCING IT AS THE MATERIAL IN THIS CHAPTER IS STUDIED.

> *The practice of remembering oneself is the master key to Gurdjieff's teaching. It is the Alpha and Omega, the threshold that must be passed at the outset and crossed and recrossed time and again. It is also the musical "silent pause" of complete realization, since any man capable of reaching it would know in their entirety the inner and outer relationships of which it consists. He would be completely himself and able at last to take his true place in the Universe.*
>
> *It must also be said that remembering oneself admits of an infinite number of approaches . . . it has certain definite degrees and stages and there is always more in it than we can ever grasp.*
>
> *Yet, beneath all its multiple forms we can savour again and again the unique taste of this fundamental experience. Nothing else matters . . . the ability to remember oneself is our birthright, it needs first to be discovered and thereafter cultivated . . . once again order is established . . . now the "I" no longer dreams . . . [this is] a new way of being. My attention is no longer the same, its power increases, its subtlety and its freedom both enlarge and enliven it.*
>
> —Henri Tracol, *The Taste For Things That Are True*, 114-117.

The Focus of This Chapter

The enneagram is an ancient spiritual symbol which existed long before Christianity or Buddhism. Mister Gurdjieff introduced it to the West. It is an engineering schematic of the actions of what he refers to as the "Law of Seven" and the "Law of Three," how they interact together to form all worlds, how they work within the *octaves** which compose our world, and how they work in the body, both physically and metaphysically.

The inner triangle represents the Law of Three, which is the main focus of this chapter. Within this schematic may also be found ways of understanding the relationship between our Creator and human beings. The purpose of this chapter, although the material is difficult and demanding, is to consider our relationship with the Divine according to the science of metaphysics, and not according to faith alone. Thus, this material appeals to reason and logic, and is of necessity more intellectual. The effort required to understand the enneagram material is the struggle to understand ourselves in relation to the great universe and our part in the creation and maintenance of our worlds; it exercises the intellectual center more than it is used to in its ordinary comfort zone. This struggle is in accordance with what Mister Gurdjieff has called "the Third Being-Obligonian Striving" (of which there are five) and which says: "The conscious striving to know ever more and more about the laws of world-creation and world-maintenance" (*Beelzebub's Tales to His Grandson*, 352).

The word "obligonian" suggests a lawful obligation on the part of those whose wish is to serve the will of God, to learn about those laws which govern the maintenance of the creation, and the part we may play in maintaining it. While I understand little about what the enneagram reveals in this respect, what follows is my struggle to understand more.

Three Essential Properties of the Self

That which remembers is in the body and is in the process of awakening; self remembering is the process by which it awakens and can then observe what it is not. Three forces are available for awakening: Presence, Attention, and Being. Presence and Attention are aspects of Being, qualities of Being. It is the development of these aspects which allows the Being to awaken. These aspects are developed by invocation: Presence is invoked by self remembering; Attention is invoked by self observation. The more persistent the invocation of these two essential qualities or aspects, the more the Being develops. This is called "the Practice of Presence." The body is meant to serve as an objective feedback mechanism to orient the Being in the present. The orientation which this practice provides gives the Being the following crucial information for operating efficiently in all circumstances and realities:

1. Who am I?
2. Where am I?
3. What is needed and wanted now?

According to Mister E.J. Gold, persistent Attention on the body alters the body from a merely biological, mechanical machine into a transformational instrument; the body is awakened to its higher function:

> We know that the essential self has two—and only two— genuine powers: the will of attention and presence, and that these two acts of will are sufficient forces in the awakening of the human biological machine, responding as it does to the compelling pressure of attention by coming to life . . . the Creation [the body. RH] could be brought to life by the power of attention . . . this would cause it to begin to function as a transformational apparatus.
>
> —E.J. Gold. *Life in the Labyrinth*, 133.

The Being develops and matures by the development of Presence and Attention; the body is the medium of transformation. When the Being is sufficiently fed, via impressions as a result of conscious Attention to impressions, it is able to become the "inner active element." Only then can the Being's essential nature, which is non-judgmental love, manifest more freely. The more fully developed the two essential Being-aspects of Presence and Attention become, the more the Being's essential nature of non-judgmental love manifests. Unless I fully inhabit the body, sensing the whole body, "I" am merely an idea, a recoil from reality.

An Inner Alchemy

In the enneagram, there is an outer circle and an inner triangle which represent, as Mister Gurdjieff taught us, the Law of Seven and the Law of Three. But this tells us virtually nothing about their practical significance. It is mere labeling, something the formatory apparatus can do with no trouble. But Being-understanding has to come from another source entirely. For many years, I have not been able to penetrate the practical meaning of this inner triangle. But the struggle to write this book, and therefore to understand more about the practice of self remembering, has brought many new revelations. One of them is the significance of this enneagram structure for our work.

There are a multitude of ways one may view the enneagram, many levels of meaning. It is a complete teaching, Mister Gurdjieff told us. But I am concerned here only with what I can understand and verify for myself, not what others may have concluded. So what I have to say on this subject is limited by my own ignorance. I do not know, therefore I depend upon personal experience, revelation, inspiration, and intuition. You must struggle to find out for yourself and understand; you must verify.

Taken in this way, it is possible to see this inner triangle as revealing something crucial about self remembering, without which understanding self remembering remains incomplete. When self remembering includes only self and other—split Attention or expanded Attention, with an arrow pointing in two directions—it is an incomplete relationship. It lacks a third force— the Law of Three—which can reconcile two opposing forces and thus create a third possibility, a new world of Being, combining the two forces into something new. This is the inner alchemy, the transmutation of forces. It is this mysterious third force which makes energy transformation possible. Real life occurs only in the presence of this third Being-force. It is this which I wish to consider with you here.

So, what can this reveal of a practical nature for me? It is not enough to remember myself as "I am" or even to include the other as "you are." Unless in this moment of self consciousness I also remember "It is," there is not a fulfillment of the inner work triad and therefore less movement and inner change. This inclusion of three forces together is third-stage self remembering.

What is "It?" Well, "It" may be God. "It" may be non-judgmental love, which Christ tells us is God. "It" may be the Work or simply Being-consciousness aware of itself. Or "It" may be the guru. In his school, Mister Lee has pointed to this level of self remembering, this inclusion of the third force in self remembering; he has given us the "remembrance practice," which is to remember the guru and myself always and in everything. And added to this practice he has given us the practice of remembering the name of God—in the case of our school: Yogi Ramsuratkumar; if I were Christian, Lord Jesus Christ. There are many names of God—like Lord Krishna . . . the list goes on. But you see what this does to the practice of self remembering, this third stage of remembrance? Ultimately, as Attention grows and matures into witness consciousness, this form of remembrance becomes simply Being-consciousness aware of itself as Presence, both in and beyond the body.

Third Force

The inner work triad has at one corner of its base "I Am" (between mi-fa). At the other corner of its base stands "You Are" (between sol-la), which is the arrow going in two directions, but horizontally, on the level of the Earth—the outer circle, the body. Add to this the apex of the triangle, "It Is" (at do), and now God, the third force, the "Holy Reconciling," has entered into the relationship with man at the descending interval do-si (descending from the *Ray of Creation** into the world of the human).

The above and the below unite. The Work tells us that man was created to act as a receiver and transmitter, to receive energy from above, to step it down by passing it through the human biological instrument—which is in its higher function a transformational instrument—and step it down so that it may be received and utilized by the Earth. Mister E.J. Gold teaches that unwavering Attention on the body changes it from simply a biological mechanism into a transformational instrument—it awakens to its higher function; in this way the practice of Presence is a practice of whole body enlightenment. Man is a feeding apparatus meant in his conscious state to feed upon that which is below and to feed that which is above—a mutual "law of reciprocal maintenance." He feeds and is fed. The conscious assimilation of impressions without inner reaction to what is received—taking no position regarding the arising of phenomena—feeds the Being. This requires a stable and persistent Presence and Attention. This kind of inner stability is impossible for a very long time, but it is the struggle to remain present in the now of the body which develops stability. *The destination is the present—it must be constantly renewed with every breath or the connection is lost.*

> *Until it is understood that it is not a question of being here now, but being here more, we won't be able to do anything to improve our situation.*
>
> —E. J. Gold, *Life in the Labyrinth*, 199.

Given this understanding of the inner triangle of the enneagram, the Christian communion ceremony takes on an added significance which was understood in the early Christian mystery schools but whose significance has been lost in the outer world. When Christ tells his disciples, "This (wine) is my blood, drink of me; this (bread or wafer) is my body, eat of me. This ye do in remembrance of me," what is now possible to understand is that this is a teaching on the transformation of lower substances into higher and finer substances to feed what is above us, and to create in oneself a higher Being-body, or the body of Christ. In the communion, there is the triad of the body and the blood forming the base of the triangle, and Christ or guru, the remembrance of the Higher, is at the apex of the triangle. It is possible to see this as a technique of self remembering given to the early Christian schools.

But the only way this transformation of substances can happen within is by conscious labor. That is, one must consciously remember to include the third force in self remembering to complete the inner work triad—which is the world of Being. It is in this level of self remembering that the Being is most well fed, grows, develops, and reaches maturity. Then one does not act alone inside. When the arrow of self remembering moves only in two directions, still one is alone inside. The result is a feeling of incompletion, the feeling that somehow something is still missing. For years I did not know what that "something" was; yet the enneagram and the guru were both pointing in the same direction: above me, something higher than me, a force beyond my comprehension which I could serve only when I remembered both self, other, and higher or third force. This third stage of remembrance invokes the Higher, invites the Higher to interact with the lower. The more persistent this invocation, the greater the chance of the "visitation" of the Holy into the ordinary existence. Now there is yet a further possible understanding of the law of invocation: "Where two or more are gathered in my name, there will I be also." (Matthew 18:20)

By adding this third force to one's conscious labor, one issues an invitation to our Creator to enter into the human relationship, into the human biological instrument, and to use this instrument for its will, not my own will. Suddenly one is no longer alone and never will be again. When one acts as the sole agent within, there is a great loneliness of the spirit, a separation grief which leads to heartbreak, which nothing but God can heal. It is this mysterious Being-longing, the unspoken heartbreak of separation, which leads one finally to bow down and surrender self-importance. And then this Holy enters into the relationship by silent conscious invitation. The silent invitation to the Holy is remembrance done in a consciously relaxed body. Relaxation is the key. Non-judgmental love will not ever force itself, is not aggressive, not violent or judgmental, does not insist, ever. It is a "lamb" and it enters only when the invitation is issued. The use of the word "lamb" here is a reference to the Biblical injunction that the lion and the lamb be made to lie down together—with the additional assumption that the lion will not consume the lamb when a certain inner work is accomplished. This work is the lawful result of a sustained Practice of Presence. A consciously relaxed body issues the invitation in silence; the Divine responds lawfully to this silent invitation. This remembrance is the healing and transformational force in human life within. It creates what Mister Gurdjieff calls a "third world," or "the world of man," and which I call "the world of Being." Only humans may create this third world, a world within, the world of the Being. *I am* includes the conscious connection with God.

> *The Speed of Light*
>
> *Love is the speed of light.*
> *The Absolute is love.*
> *The Absolute is the speed of light.*
> *The speed of light is stillness and silence.*
> *The Absolute is stillness and silence.*
> *Love is stillness and silence.*
> *Where is stillness?*
> *Between motion.*
> *Where is silence?*
> *Between sound.*
> *Where is the Absolute?*
> *Between motion and sound.*
> *Silence between every sound.*
> *Stillness between every motion.*
> —Life in the Labyrinth, 140.

Non-Interference

When the Sufis say, "Take no position regarding the arising of phenomena," what is being taught is the practice of non-interference, or in Work terms what is called "non-identification," which occurs in a consciously relaxed body, which implies an inner stability possible only when the Being is the active force. Only when there is this complete act of conscious self remembering is it possible to not interfere with the incoming impressions, which may then become the "third Being-food" of which Mister Gurdjieff speaks. This act of self remembering is the basis of non-judgmental love, or impersonal love. What is absent then is self-importance. Don Juan Matus, the Yaqui shaman and teacher of Carlos Castaneda, has this to say about self-importance:

> *What weakens us is feeling offended by the deeds and misdeeds of other men. Our self-importance requires that we spend most of our lives offended by someone. Without self-importance we are invulnerable.*
>
> —in Castenada, *The Fire from Within*, 12.

Invulnerable to what? Well, one thing is the identification with the intellectual-emotional complex. The great irony of self remembering is that as one practices it, one's self-importance diminishes. "I" becomes aware of itself in a vastly larger context than the mere individuated self. It becomes part of an infinitely larger machinery which creates and destroys, feeds and is fed upon, a system of "reciprocal maintenance" in which it serves a small but not insignificant role, but only so long as I am able to remember myself. Then Attention expands to include more than the small self, the egoic self.

The Being is a point in a field, a microcosm in a macrocosm, a conscious field of sensitive clear light awareness within an infinite field of sensitive awareness, a charged particle within a charged field. When I am present, the particle remains charged and is able to carry the charge from the greater field, both a receiving post and a transmitting post. The moment one identifies, the field goes black and the particle loses its charge.

The Two Keys to Self Remembering

There are two real keys to transformation in self remembering. The first is the expanding, or splitting, of Attention so that there is awareness of the environment, of oneself externally, relaxing the body within its space, and the awareness of one's inner reactions at the same time. This conscious act cannot be overemphasized. It is splitting Attention, expanding it to include more than just the small self. When this expanded Attention is enacted, one is able to catch inner reactions to impressions (associations, judgments, labeling and categorizing, explaining) before they reach the will. One remains more objective, relaxed, and observant without being "taken" by identification with the inner reaction. One is able to remain present to the Presence within, which gives it the opportunity to feed and develop, to grow and mature. The Being in this state becomes the active principle within, because there is no interference with incoming impressions. One is able to gather impressions of mechanical reactive processes without being taken by them. On the other hand, one may simply be unable to resist the pull of identification, but able to remain alert to being "taken" and observe the process by which identification takes place. This gathering of such impressions is what gives force and strength to the wish to remain present.

The second key to transformation in self remembering is the remembrance of the guru or God or love, and bringing this third force into the act of self observation, sensing the Divine from Above while remembering myself externally and within— all at the same time. This is third-stage self remembering. It is not as difficult as it sounds when trying to describe it, and the result is an inner freedom which cannot be described. It must be experienced: a delicate, subtle sense of alignment. A certain joy may arise with this experience. One is given a "free look" and is allowing "a look from Above" at the same time. One becomes real food in the food chain up the Ray of Creation to our Creator. In this level of expansion, the "I" disappears into the whole, the point merges with the field. Then there will be the contraction, or recoil, into "myself" again, which contraction is fear. Love expands, fear contracts.

So right now, with the book open here, take a moment: with both feet on the floor and the spine in a good posture, consciously bringing Attention down to the abdominal area, locate the sensation of breath and sense the whole body; relax the body; broaden the focus of awareness to include both the inner Presence and the outer impressions. Now open at the top of the head and the front of the body, to sense this offering of the body to something higher, something above you in scale. Sense this invitation to the Divine without thinking about it, but only by sensation and awareness. Just for a moment, become *prasad*. Become an offering. *Prasad* is an offering made to the guru or God, often food, and laid at the guru's feet as a sign of gratitude, service, and humility. And this offering of the self is not an offering of something perfect. I offer myself exactly as I am, with all my flaws, all of my errors held out in honesty and devotion as food.

Intervals, Shocks and Octaves

There is one more thing about the enneagram and what it may tell me about self remembering—Tracol indicates that the levels of possible meaning regarding self remembering are infinite, and this appears to be the case with the enneagram as well. Nevertheless, struggling to understand more may produce important and helpful insights. For example, there is the curious placement of this inner triangle within the outer circle of this diagram.

In the outer circle of the enneagram, there appear intervals, which are those places in any endeavor where the forward motion stops, runs out of steam so to speak. These intervals appear at the two points of the base of the inner triangle, at the points 3 and 6, or between the notes mi and fa (point 3) and between sol and la (point 6). However, Ouspensky tells us that this second interval, between the notes sol and la, represents what may be called "a lawful incongruity," or as he explains it,

> *The apparent placing of the interval [sol-la. RH] in its wrong place itself shows to those who are able to read the symbol what kind of "shock is required to the passage of si to do." Mister Gurdjieff said, "The final substance in the process of the food octave is the substance si ("hydrogen" 12 in the third scale), which needs an "additional shock" in order to pass into a new do.*
>
> —*In Search of the Miraculous,* 292.

In other words, the way I struggle to understand this is that in order for any line of action to continue in a straight line without deviation or retardation, or in order for incoming energy to be fully transformed in the body so that it may become higher Being-food, there must be an inner force—conscious labor—which carries the energy across this sol-la interval to strike a new chord, a higher octave. This is also true of the mi-fa interval, at which air (the first Being-food) enters the organism. It is at this point, mi-fa, that the first shock occurs, the shock of air or breath. It is said that this shock is mechanical, unconscious—but it need not be if one is engaged here in the Practice of Presence, in which one is aware of the breath. The point sol-la, we are told, is the point at which impressions enter the octave. Impressions are what Mister Gurdjieff called "the second Being-food."

> *The first of these . . . (conscious) shocks belongs to the intake of impressions and the reception of them and the digestion of them. This shock is called the First Conscious Shock . . . In the Enneagram the left angle of the . . . triangle refers to the First Conscious Shock . . . impressions do not give the shock in the same way as Air does unless they are taken in consciously . . . This is the place where we must digest everything that happens to us . . .*
> —Maurice Nicoll. *Psychological Commentaries,* 390.

Put in ordinary language, there comes a point in any endeavor, let's take marriage as an example, when one may begin to feel a loss of force and one observes that the initial energy which carried the endeavor for a ways is diminishing; this point in the enneagram may be seen as the mi-fa interval. At this point, unless there is a conscious intervention on my part, what the Work calls "conscious labor"—that is, I remember myself and begin to observe myself—the endeavor may begin to turn back upon itself and become quite the opposite of what one originally intended—the marriage becomes a war and divorce may be the result . . . to continue the example of marriage.

But the enneagram, indicated by the position of the lower left angle of the inner triangle, shows that the shock necessary to accomplish this move across this interval does not occur at the point si-do in the enneagram (where Mister Gurdjieff tells us that an additional shock is required), but at the point sol-la: a lawful incongruity. Why is it "in its wrong place" (as Ouspenky notes above)? One possible way of understanding this is to see it as pointing to the role of self remembering in serving this law of reciprocal maintenance. The first food, which is our ordinary organic food intake, is digested and assimilated mechanically, requiring no conscious participation on my part at all in order to perform its lawful function. At the point mi-fa in the enneagram, a shock is required for this food octave to continue without deviation, and this is provided by air, which is the first Being-food. When the food air enters the body, I may be conscious and remember myself even here. I may remember the breath here. This is another aspect of first-stage self remembering. Breath and relaxation are essential tools in the invocation of Presence and Attention.

Continuing with the example of marriage to help understand what the enneagram is showing us, the relationship continues in a more or less straight line in its octave until it reaches the point mi-fa in the octave, when one begins to sense that the endeavor is losing its force, or its so-called spark. There is a stagnation. One finds the marriage "in a rut" so to speak. There is an inner shift from desire to indifference. The original energy has become stagnant or used up. At that point conscious labor is called for, in the form of self remembering and self observation; it is self observation which begins to reveal oneself to oneself. The result at this point is conscious suffering. One begins to bear one's own cross. Something begins to awaken which was not present before. I begin to see that the suffering which I once blamed others for is in fact originating in me.

This shock provides a new energy in the relationship. I see my own selfishness and I begin to see and consciously consider the feelings of others as well as my own in order that the endeavor might move to a new level of maturity, less selfish. Otherwise, it is war all the time, or else the friendship disintegrates, or the relationship simply stagnates and a kind of indifference results. Arnaud Desjardins describes this new level of maturity as the move from "self only" to the level of "self–others": I remember myself while at the same time considering the other—her feelings, her needs, her path toward awakening—and I begin to consciously serve her. There is a shock which moves the relationship across the mi-fa interval.

But then there is a second interval indicated in the enneagram, at the point sol-la. And it is at this point when what is called "the first conscious shock" must enter in order to keep the energy in motion in a straight line. To accomplish the move from si to do, which is accomplished by the Divine, conscious labor must enter in. That is, the second Being-food, impressions, must be taken in consciously in order to be transformed into something useful to the Divine.

But the interval is placed where it apparently does not belong—at sol-la. Perhaps (I do not know for sure), this could indicate that it is at this point that I must remember myself in relationship with others, the second angle at the base of the inner triangle, whose point is at sol-la. And at this point one brings into the triad the most Holy, the guru or God. Ouspensky tells us:

It was pointed out in the cosmic octave [working in reverse from man's octave, do-re-mi; thus, the cosmic octave works do-si-la. RH] in relation to the "interval" *do-si that* this passage is accomplished by the will of the Absolute *[my emphasis. RH]*.

—*In Search of the Miraculous*, 291.

When self remembering happens at this point, with conscious placement of Attention at the heart/solar plexus region so as not to interfere with the passage of energy food into the next higher octave, only then may the energy be purified—devoid of identification with impressions—and self remembering and ruthlessly honest self observation provide the impetus for God to move the energy across the next interval at si-do.

To carry the marriage example further, in ordinary terms this means that at some point in any relationship, friendship, or energetic configuration—and it is the same for individuals as for organizations and nations—there comes a point where the endeavor either begins to lose force, energy, and dwindles, or something must happen to elevate it to a new level. Whereas a certain level of growth and maturity occurred to move it across the mi-fa interval, now something further, something more is asked of me in order for the relationship to continue to grow in a straight line. The relationship, and the beings involved in it, must continue to grow and mature, or the result is collapse or stagnation. At this point, one must act consciously. Continued self remembering and self observation lead to a deeper understanding and insight. Intentional suffering occurs as one sees the strategies to avoid relationship and to avoid growing up. One must begin to take new responsibility for unconscious, habitual manifestations.

I suffer myself. I see how I withdraw my love and escape from the present, from relationship. I begin to act unselfishly, but at a new level. To continue Arnaud Desjardins' explanation, the Being's inner growth now moves from "self–others" to an *inner shift in context* and this shift may be described as "others–self." That is, I act not only to consider the feelings of others, but now *I place their feelings before my own*. I act selflessly. Here is where worship and adoration may enter into the marriage. One becomes a servant of the marriage; one becomes a servant of life, a mature Being. There is selflessness and sacrifice then, for the good of the other, regardless of the cost to oneself. This is the point in a relationship where the level of respect for the other increases dramatically, and is accompanied with a similar increase in self-worth. It is this level of maturity which prepares one, and the relationship itself, to move to the point si-do in the octave, where the Divine enters. One must be prepared for this descending grace to fulfill the relationship, or it will be squandered, wasted, because the participants are not prepared, are not at the level to use this blessing force for the good of others, without the *contamination** of egoic desires. When this grace descends into human life, the marriage, for example, becomes a conscious instrument of Divine will.

All relationships are persistent to the degree that the beings involved have the same expansion.
—Thaddeus Golas, 58.

It is at this point, do-si in the descending octave or the Ray of Creation from our Creator, and si-do in the ascending octave from the human, that the Higher and the lower, the Divine and the human, meet. At this point, a relationship may be entered into between the human and our Creator—but only if I have remembered myself and am in place when they meet at si-do (third-stage self remembering). Otherwise, if I am unconscious there, I am unable to serve Divine needs, I cannot receive Divine influences, and I miss the opportunity to place myself under the will of our Creator. I do not issue the invitation to our Creator to enter into conscious relationship with me at si because I am not present in a relaxed body when this occurs.

Eating Impressions

It is just here, at this point sol-la, where a "special effort" is called for. I call this special effort "eating impressions." This is the point where impressions enter into the organism. There are two ways to take in impressions: mechanically or consciously. Here we speak of consciously taking in impressions. The way that I understand this effort is that when the impression enters, the first inner effort is to observe my automatic, unconscious, mechanical reactions to it; I observe my judgments. But it becomes a kind of "super effort" (in Work terms) when I do not identify with those judgments. Furthermore, I do not express my negativity in the form of outer show: words, facial expressions, or bodily indications. I sense the whole body and keep the body relaxed, I sense the breath, and I do not move away from the present, here now: I remember myself. In other words, I "eat" my negativity.

When asked what the source of her energy was, Madame de Salzmann replied: "I use my negativity." Now, we can appreciate that there are more levels of meaning to her statement. With those words she indicates, in subtle manner, the special effort needed at the point sol-la to transform crude energy into finer Being-food and food to feed the guru and God. "God" is attracted to the source of real food, wishing to be fed. In this way, conscience is also fed. [*Please see Chapter 12 for further information on what is meant by not expressing negativity, in the discussion on conscious management of the survival instinct.*] One might even say, very tentatively and humbly, that conscience is the will of God. One might also say that conscience is our direct link to our Creator; thus, when conscience is fed, God is fed.

Entering into Relationship with the Divine

To continue, I must be present at sol-la in order for the Divine to enter into relationship with the lower at si. However, when I remember myself at sol-la, now I issue the invitation for our Creator to enter into the human realm, to enter into the body and to perform the inner work of transformation. I make myself available to the higher will by entering this interval in a state of active passivity (conscious labor). I provide consciously purified food that feeds the Divine, thus it is attracted. That is, I am conscious and I do not interfere with the work of our Creator. It may enter here because there is no identification with incoming impressions and no interference with the movement of energy as it completes the inner octave—there is an inner silence, accepting what is, as it is, here and now, which allows for a space to be made in which something higher may reside for a moment. Then the body becomes a transformational instrument. Only now, at this point in the enneagram and in oneself, is conscious love—non-judgmental love—possible. Our Creator comes in the form of non-judgmental love.

At this point "doing" can happen—I cannot "do" (as Mister Gurdjieff so often points out) but "Thy will" is "done" in me. Non-judgmental love may occur only when "I am" and am "not-doing," not interfering with incoming impressions—which is energy—which is Divine, and knows what to do and where to go in the body in order for transformation of energy or impressions to occur, if I stay in place inside and do not interfere. Please note that the only thing which has changed in me is my relationship to these inner forces. I no longer resist them. I accept, I allow, and I relax into love. I mind my own business—remembering myself/ observing myself—and God takes care of its business. Here arises the possibility to love myself.

I have speculated here as to why the interval sol-la is in the "wrong place" (according to Ouspensky) in the enneagram. This is mere speculation on my part, struggling to understand more. But Madame de Salzmann has given further clues as to what is required of me at this point in the enneagram in her discussion #86, *First and second conscious shocks*:

> In order to provoke a stop, suffering is necessary so that a third force can appear. Then the attention becomes voluntary—I wish not to be taken, I wish to remain free ... The degree of this will of attention produces an opening of my body to a finer energy. Everything depends on this opening. I need to feel the energy in my mind and in my body simultaneously with the same force. My attention needs to last and not diminish.
>
> —The Reality of Being, 185.

For those of us who are engaged in the Practice of Presence, or self remembering, this last statement about the Attention needing to last is significant, because one learns quickly that herein lies the problem: Attention is weak and cannot last long at all. Thus the struggle to remain present is crucial, because that struggle develops and strengthens Attention. And it is this struggle which is called for at the sol-la interval, where impressions enter. Here one struggles to maintain Attention and not be taken in judgment or identification, so that Attention may last longer. Mister E.J. Gold noted that it is not just how *often* I remember to be present, but how *long*. It appears that the duration of Attention is crucial to bridge the long gap in the enneagram between sol and la (numbers 5 and 6—the two longest gaps are between mi-fa and sol-la, thus the need for a new energy to bridge them), thereby creating the energy for the second conscious shock (from our Creator) at si-do.

I am indebted to my friend Lee Van Laer for his help in my struggle with this portion of the enneagram. It was he who pointed out that placing the left base of the triangle, at point 6, was practical, in that it indicates the necessity of *a balanced work effort for the harmonious development of all three centers at once.* This placement creates a visibly balanced structure. Whereas, if the left angle of the triangle were placed at si-do (number 8) it would be a completely unbalanced structure which made no sense and was in no way harmonious. Madame also indicates this need for a balanced, simultaneous effort in more than one center here, at the second conscious shock. She continues:

> *All the centers are involved. If one reaches fa, it can draw the others toward fa. All the centers must be in front of the interval for the intensity of vibration to increase. The relation between the centers is the shock necessary to pass the interval, which will never be passed without it. In our working on this relation, a force appears, and we then feel a vibration that opens the door to a different level.*
>
> —*The Reality of Being*, 185.

So it appears that the intensity of vibration is equal in some way to the intensity of the effort required for one to hold Attention in place when impressions enter, and not to be taken in identification or judgment, but to remain present. When she speaks of fa, or the first shock, the same may be said for sol, or the first conscious shock. These are the points where the effort of self remembering is so important. Without it, if one identifies with the incoming impression, all energy is consumed and lost, there is no increase in the inner vibratory rate, and the intensity to bridge the interval sol-la, preparing to meet the descending Divine love current, is not available. Finally, Madame continues:

> *In proceeding further with the octave, the question of the second conscious shock can appear only when I have been consciously present for a sufficiently long time. In this effort of Presence, my feeling warms up and is transformed. It purifies itself [see Lee Van Laer's enneagram diagram at the beginning of the chapter, where point 6 indicates suffering, and point 7 purification. RH] and my emotions become positive [through the struggle with impressions—only this purification of energy can meet with the pure descending Divine energy. RH]. But this does not last; my emotions fall back and again become as usual. This shows that what in me observes, what watches, has no will. The interval between si and do is very difficult to pass.*
>
> *I seek to be present to what I am, but I do not feel it. It does not touch me. I feel my incapacity: I have no feeling, no substance, that would allow me to become conscious of myself. In this conflict a feeling appears that is different from my habitual emotions. The question of myself has a*

new urgency . . . This second shock—an emotional shock—changes the whole character of a person.

When we can remember ourselves, be open to ourselves, for long enough, we are put to the test by the intervention of the subjective "I" in the face of other people's manifestations toward us. At the moment the impression is received by the mind, I react . . . I identify with the form projected by my thought. So, if I wish to go further, I need to be shocked, shaken, by seeing the selfish reaction of my ego, defending itself out of fear of being denied. In order to be free from this fear, I have to experience it, to wholly live with everything it entails.

With a second conscious shock, it is possible that consciousness opens and we see reality . . . At this moment I realize that my emotion is no longer the same. There is no closing, no negation, I do not refuse, I do not accept. With this vigilance, which does not choose, a new feeling appears and a new understanding, not born from opposites . . . a feeling of unity, of being.

—*The Reality of Being,* 185-186.

Now, the inner work-triad is completed with the inclusion of self (between mi-fa), other (between sol-la), and our Creator (at do). This third-stage self remembering allows our Creator, the "Absolute," to accomplish its will, to pass the higher energy down the scale from do to si, where it may be taken in consciously by conscious man and stepped down to feed the developing Earth and all of creation.

To follow the marriage example to its logical conclusion in explaining the movement of the enneagram—which is always in motion, a living thing—the more one acts in a selfless way, the more the longing to give up one's own will to something higher increases. The maturing of self remembering and self observation brings one to this level: Not my will, but Thy will be done. Through self observation, I have suffered myself and my behavior to the point of surrender. Just here is where the great work task comes into play: to bear the unpleasant manifestations of others—our mate—without identification with inner reaction, complaint, or outer show, and to express no negativity: to eat impressions. Now one fully utilizes intentional suffering. It is at this point that one picks up one's own cross and begins to carry it, not laying one's faults on others as in blame and justification, but suffering them quietly, without show or complaint. One takes responsibility for one's inner life, reactions, thoughts and emotions, habits, flaws, and lays these at the feet of our Creator, or the guru. One sees clearly that one cannot do it alone. One then offers oneself up in sacrificial love. When one brings the Divine or the guru into the relationship, it places the marriage on a new footing, it raises it to a new level, or it begins a new octave of service and sacrifice; it moves it across the sol-la interval; it becomes a conscious offering to the Divine, a different kind of Prasad. It allows the marriage to grow to its ultimate human maturity, its full flowering, to increase in understanding and non-judgmental love, to become selfless, and to serve something greater than itself. Arnaud Desjardins, to complete his scale of the growth of the inner Being, describes this note as the move from "others–self" to "others only." The individuated self disappears into love. It allows non-judgmental love to be passed through the transformational apparatus of the marriage and out into the Creation. All who touch such a union are changed in some way by it—are affected, though they do not know why or how. Instead of constant fighting, or indifference, there is an outer harmony because an inner harmony has been established. The marriage becomes a vehicle for grace and mercy. It is conscious labor and *voluntary or intentional suffering** in the form of self remembering and self observation which produce this effect on individuals and relationships. The enneagram explains precisely the energetic demands which make the transformation of an individual and a relationship possible—what is required of me at any given point in order to keep the marriage or friendship alive.

At the same time, when I engage in such a struggle to consider others before myself, the power of Presence and Attention grows, becomes free of identification and self-importance. Humility emerges from this practice. When "I" becomes totally vulnerable, without defense or interference, what is left is Presence alone: consciousness—a conscious, sensitive field of clear light awareness. My guru Mister Lee, in his devotional poetry to his Master, Yogi Ramsuratkumar, has written about this expanded Attention and remembrance of God in this way:

Whatever I am doing in the outer/world, no matter, sitting, writing,/sleeping, eating, working, anything/and everything, at the very/same time I am also in full pranam/ to You, and still at the same time,/circumambulating You and Your/Holy objects and spaces./ . . . Now some would say

that two/things or more cannot be done/at the same time,
impossible,/ . . . Are we not multidimensional beings . . . ?/
There is no paradox and no separation./There is a seamless
Unity, a Oneness . . .
—Lee Lozowick. *Intimate Secrets of A True Heart Son*: 245.

Once I have aligned myself with the Above, with the guru and our Creator, many things will arise within. Every negative "i" and self-sabotaging mechanism will react with strength to regain control of Attention and maintain its supremacy in me. I must be prepared to deal with and move through every kind of inner negativity now, maintaining a constant focus on the guru and God and not wavering in my commitment to growth and to trust and faith in guru, God, and the Work. This may be a most difficult inner period of "breakdown before breakthrough" (Werner Erhard) in which every bit of my work will be tested and called upon to sustain me. This is intentional suffering.

Here again, the help and support of a group, a sangha, and even a guru are most useful. A practical and sensible intelligence is called for throughout spiritual practice. One makes use of all available help. I may even require professional help to work through old material which I have not dealt with thoroughly before. This was the case with me. But thanks to the guru's blessing force I found most excellent help, all that I needed, to work through this—what is called "the dark night of the soul." It is painful, demanding, and then something gives way for something new to emerge. Such suffering is both necessary and lawful; it is the way in which identification with the personality is broken. It frees one from the slavery and fascination with me-myself, which is a collection of memories, or personal history—a description of me built from my personal history. There is a gradual shift within: what was passive (Being) becomes more active, and what was active (personality) becomes passive, a source of food for the growth of Being. A kind of softness eventually develops in this process, in which the front of the body becomes open and vulnerable to creation, creating a sense of trust and vulnerability in which the body becomes prasad offered as food to God and the guru; there is a kind of humble gratitude and even joy in this softening process.

> *All of us are born with a set of instinctive fears—of falling, of the dark, of lobsters, of falling on lobsters in the dark, or of speaking before a Rotary Club, and of the words "Some Assembly Required."*
> —Dave Barry

Becoming Prasad

Beloved Master, I lay the life of
this body at Your Holy feet; this
is the only Prasad I have for You
so I bring it here and lay it

before You, that You and Your Father
may be nourished; this offering
to the Guru is food for His life.
It is a small and poor gift, but

You are able to turn dross to gold,
I have seen it. You have conquered
Death itself and You can make use
of such a humble gift as this life.

Every thought is Your Prasad,
every emotion is Your Prasad,
every breath is Your Prasad Master.
Surrender it in Love;

make me Your food.
Consume me.

—Red Hawk, *Mother Guru*, 125

CHAPTER 10

The Solar Plexus, Heart Center, Abdomen

I.

Jeanne de Salzmann. *The Reality of Being.*

The quality of the energy of the lower centers must correspond to the vibrations of the higher centers. Otherwise, the relation is not made and the lower centers do not express the action of the higher on the level of life . . . As a result, they do not have any conscious activity and do not feel any need to be purified . . . (51) everything that is below holds us back. It must all be purified. (52)

   Inside, my attention . . . is always passive . . . my body and my functions are active. . . I have to feel the necessity to change this relation so that my body and my functions accept a state of voluntary passivity. This can take place only if I actively situate the center of gravity of my attention . . . (139)

   A certain sensation appears and, with the need to let it spread, there is a letting go that takes place by itself. . . an

essential Presence makes itself felt in my whole body . . . A
conscious attention, coming in part from a new feeling, relates
the sensation and the letting go. (139)

At the beginning I have a tendency to experience this
sensation predominantly in the solar plexus or in the head.
But with the letting go, the sensation expands and takes
the form of a whole presence that is rooted in the abdomen.
Gurdjieff always pointed to this place as the center of gravity
of the being, the point where the second body is attached to
the first. I let my energy flow toward this center of gravity,
which is a support for the entire upper part of the body. It is
also the support for my thought and feeling . . . (139-140)

I wish to trust life, trust this irresistible power centered
in my abdomen . . . the abdomen must be filled with the
force of the whole body . . . The muscles below the navel are
lightly tensed. This brings a certain concentration of force
at this place, which needs to be activated by energy coming
from all the parts . . . the abdomen supports the whole upper
body . . . The force from above descends toward the center of
gravity that supports it. (143)

II.

Ramana Maharshi. *The Spiritual Teaching of Ramana Maharshi.*

If one enquires as to where in the body the thought "I" rises
first, one would discover that it rises in the heart. That is the
place of the mind's origin. (5)

[Questioner:] What is the nature of the heart?

The sacred texts describing it say: Between the two nipples, below the chest and above the abdomen, there are six organs of different colors. One of them resembling the bud of a water lily and situated two digits to the right is the heart . . . All the psychic nerves (nadis) depend upon it. It is the abode of the vital forces, the mind and the light (of consciousness) . . . the meaning of the word heart (hrdayam) is the Self (Atman) . . . When it is realized as it is, there is no scope for discussions about its location inside the body or outside. (23)

[Questioner:] But Sri Bhagavan has specified a particular place for the Heart within the physical body, that it is in the chest, two digits to the right from the median.

Yes, that is the center of spiritual experience as according to the testimony of Sages . . . All that you can say of the Heart is that it is the very core of your being . . . From this absolute standpoint, the Heart, Self, or Consciousness can have no particular place assigned to it in the physical body . . . (91-92)

[Questioner:] But I have heard it said by a saint that his spiritual experience is felt at the place between the eyebrows.

As I said previously, that is the ultimate and perfect Realization which transcends subject-object relation. When that is achieved, it does not matter where the spiritual experience is felt. (95)

[Questioner:] But the question is which is the correct view of the two, namely, (1) that the center of spiritual experience is the place between the eyebrows, (2) that it is the Heart?

If during sleep the experience of the Self is not felt between the eyebrows, that center cannot be called its seat without implying that the Self often forsakes its own place, which is absurd. The fact is the sadhaka may have his experience at any center or chakra on which he concentrates his mind. But for that reason that particular place of his experience does not become ipso facto the seat of the Self (96)

[Questioner:] Sri Bhagavan says that the Self may function at any of the centers or chakras while its seat is in the Heart . . .

As long as it is merely the stage of practice of concentration by fixing a place of controlling your attention, any consideration about the seat of the Self would merely be a theorization. (98-99)

[Questioner:] Why does not Sri Bhagavan direct us to practice concentration on some particular center (or) chakra?"

Yoga Sastras say that the sahasrara or the brain is the seat of the Self. Purusa Sukta declares that the Heart is its seat. To enable the sadhaka to steer clear of possible doubt, I tell him to take up the "thread" or the clue of "I"ness or "I-am"-ness and follow it up to its source. (100)

III.

Osho Rajneesh. *The Secret of Secrets.*

[Questioner:] Master Lu-tsu said: Nothing is possible without contemplation. Perceiving brings one to the goal. What has to be reversed by reflection is the self-conscious heart, which has to direct itself towards that point where the formative spirit is not yet manifest . . . One looks with both eyes at the tip of the nose, sits upright and in a comfortable position, and holds the heart to the centre in the midst of conditions. It does not necessarily mean the middle of the head, It is only a matter of fixing one's thinking on the point which lies exactly between the two eyes. Then all is well. The light is something extremely mobile. When one fixes the thought on the mid-point between the two eyes, the light streams in of its own accord. (350, 352)

The ego is called 'the self-conscious heart' . . . I am only if I think. If thinking disappears, the I also disappears . . . This I-amness, this self-conscious heart is nothing but a continuum of thoughts. It is not really an entity, it is a false entity, an illusion.... (361)

Now the practical point of the whole sutra [of Master Lu-tsu. RH]—is very simple, but try to understand it correctly, because mind wants to distort even simple things. Mind is a distorting mechanism...the mind always turns simple things into complexities. Beware of that, because the mind cannot exist with the simple...so the investment of the mind is in complexity. (363-364)

[Questioner:] One should look at the tip of one's nose.

Why?—because this helps, it brings you in line with the third eye . . . the basic is that your third eye is exactly in line with the tip of the nose—just a few inches above, but in the same line. And once you are in the line of the third eye, the attraction of the third eye . . . is so great that if you have fallen in line with it you will be pulled even against yourself. You just have to be exactly in line with it so that the attraction, the gravitation, of the third eye starts functioning . . . Suddenly you will find the gestalt has changed, because the two eyes create the duality of the world and thought, and the single eye between the two eyes creates the gaps. This is a simple method of changing the gestalt.(364)

And when you have reached the third-eye point and you are centered there and the light is flooding in, you have reached the point from which the whole creation has arisen. You have reached the formless, the unmanifest. Call it God if you will. This is the point, this is the space, from which all has arisen. This is the very seed of the whole existence. It is omnipotent, it is omnipresent, it is eternal. (375)

IV.

Chögyam Trungpa. *Shambhala: The Sacred Path of the Warrior.*

Basic goodness* is very closely connected to the idea of bodhicitta in the Buddhist tradition. Bodhi means "awake" or "wakeful" and citta means "heart," so bodhicitta is "awakened heart." Such awakened heart comes from being willing to face your state of mind . . . You should examine yourself *and ask how many times you have tried to connect with your heart, fully and truly. How often have you turned away, because you feared you might discover something terrible about yourself?... how much have you connected with yourself at all in your whole life?*

The sitting practice of meditation...is the means to rediscover basic goodness, and beyond that, it is the means to awaken the genuine heart within yourself... So through the practice of sitting still and following your breath as it goes out and dissolves, you are connecting with your heart...

When you awaken your heart in this way, you find ... that your heart is empty... If you search for awakened heart ... there is nothing there except for tenderness. You feel sore and soft, and if you open your eyes to the rest of the world, you feel tremendous sadness ... You don't feel sad because someone has insulted you or because you feel impoverished. Rather, this experience of sadness is unconditioned. It occurs because your heart is completely exposed.

The genuine heart of sadness comes from feeling that your nonexistent heart is full . . . Real fearlessness is the product of tenderness. It comes from letting the world tickle your heart, your raw and beautiful heart. You are willing to open up without resistance or shyness, and face the world. You are willing to share your heart with others. (44-46)

V.

A.H. Almaas. *Diamond Heart: Book Four.*

What exists, what is permanent, is the heart itself. The heart is beingness, an expression of Being. Being is indestructible.

It is independent of your mind. A human being is not truly realized unless he can be the courageous heart.

The courageous heart is independent of what the other person does and what the other person thinks of you. To have a courageous heart, you need to accept a certain kind of aloneness, a certain kind of independence. With the courageous heart, you are so independent that the person can do all kinds of unpleasant things but you can still see the reality. In that independence, the feeling is that you have to give constantly, regardless of what the other person does or what the situation is. (203)

VI.

Lee Lozowick. *Words of Fire & Faith.*

[Questioner]: If there is nothing inside of me that can free me, and nothing outside of me that can free me, where do I place my attention?

You know . . . that if it is the "you" whom you have become so passionately and blindly as well as lovingly and affectionately identified with, then of course no matter where "you" place "your" attention, even if it is on guru or God, it will be ultimately ineffective relative to the goal of this Path . . . As long as it is this "you" that you cling to and defend so tenaciously, inside and outside, what does it matter?

Yes, of course you can easily create all kinds of phenomena . . . but [they] . . . will only add to the mistaken belief that you are getting somewhere—like making progress towards transformation. There is such a reality as the placement of objective attention, but this "you" we are discussing can never place attention correctly, not even by accident. Because this "you" is false, so too is everything this "you" generates, even . . . love, prayer, devotion, faith, whatever. (33-34)

. . .[W]e must somehow let the Universe place our attention; in other words, when the Universe places our attention we could call this Surrender to the Will of God, for the Universe has Will, momentum, chaotic Intelligence— all quite lawful of course—but no attention. The Universe cannot have attention, although it does have Intention,* another word for Will as we are using it. In any case, it is important . . . for attention to be placed rightly. We are the Universe's (or God's, if you will) vehicles or agents for this function . . .* (34)

When we are able to allow the Will of God to animate in our field of influence, all dualities...become irrelevant and the just placement of attention finds itself attentive to whatever, wherever, and whoever...that attention can and does serve in that exact "here and now, as it is" . . . (34)

So, if we aim to live according to the Truth, the only solution, according to the context of this path that we have so ardently embraced, is to allow the Universe, or the Will of God, to place "our" attention as pure attention, and not only for random and occasional moments (although we all have to start somewhere) but ultimately . . . moment to moment to such an extreme degree that we aren't dividing and separating . . . There, at that point, we aren't even conscious that there is a difference between "our" attention—the "our" of the indentified [sic] "I," "me," "you"—and the Will of God. At that point there is only the Will of God . . . (35-36)

The Great Conundrum

Perhaps, from the six readings given above, you see the situation. Herein lies the great conundrum: it becomes obvious to anyone who has pursued the practice of self observation that it is necessary to consciously move Attention out of the mind and into the body in order to gain a more objective, non-identified view of the mind's workings. Now the very real question arises: *where* in the body is the most efficient, conscious placement of Attention? This is an investigation which every serious student must take on for oneself. Where in the body must Attention be placed so that it has a center from which to observe the mind and the emotions?

When speaking of mind here, it is the "formatory mind" (Mister Gurdjieff) or memory function of the neo-cortex which is being spoken of. This memory function is a binary computer. When Attention is given to this mind, in order to observe, it cannot be housed in that mind which I wish to observe. To observe the mind within the mind is a dead-end street; it goes nowhere and it is nearly impossible not to identify with what is observed. It is the mistake which "observing I" makes. It is the mind trying to observe itself. The computer cannot observe the operations of the computer objectively; that is, without identification. Therefore, another position outside the mind is required in order to observe the mind.

But where? There is not one single correct answer to this question. It differs from Master to Master.

This chapter begins with readings from Madame de Salzmann, Sri Ramana Maharshi, Osho Rajneesh, Chögyam Trungpa Rinpoche, Mister A.H. Almaas, and my own Master, Mister Lee Lozowick, because I have the highest regard for each of these realized masters. I do not question the level of their attainment.

And Madame de Salzmann refers to her own master, Mister George Gurdjieff, the great master of the Work. She indicates that the most efficient placement of Attention is at the abdomen. According to her, this is the point where the second body links with the first, or physical, body. She indicates that those who have only begun the investigation of where to locate Attention feel the sensation in the solar plexus, and I must confess that this is where my Attention often, but not always, wishes to go, to a point just above the navel and below where the ribcage and the breastbone intersect. It is this portion of the abdomen.

But, I have also observed Attention falling into the heart, or heart chakra. So when speaking of the solar plexus region, it is the area of the abdomen between the navel and the heart chakra, no need to get more specific. You must investigate. This is a tricky business, this chapter. I have cobbled together evidence from many sources to suggest a beginning point for investigation, not the final destination. From here, **let it settle itself**.

Let It Settle Itself

Please understand this; I am a beginner. I have said before that if one does not interfere, Attention will eventually find its own center of gravity and will settle itself (see Mister Lee's quote above). I do not want to crystallize this question as if I knew the complete and final answer to it. In fact, it may not matter where one places the Attention below the neck, just so long as it is down lower in the body, out of the mind. But one must investigate for oneself, finding where Attention naturally gravitates to in the body.

So don't worry about it; don't make it an issue or a problem. **Let it settle itself,** Buddha said. Attention will go where it is needed, when it is appropriate. Simply rest easy in the present, the now of the body, and allow the practice to do the rest.

Lee Lozowick's Instruction

Mister Lee's answer above raises some challenging questions about this entire consideration. In order to consider his answer, three things must be understood. The first thing is that when Mister Lee uses the word "our" in his answer, he is using this word in the same way that I am using "me-myself," that imaginary, intellectual construct which I have come to identify with as my very self. In fact, it is a collection of memories organized around what the Work calls a "chief feature," and which I call a "blind spot." This me-myself is a lie, and from it no possible truth can arise. Every move I make, both inner and outer, is this fabricated entity which some call "ego." This me-myself is not even rightly called an "entity," for it is in fact the very act of recoil from the present, from love, from the will of God. This me-myself is the act of recoil.

The second thing to understand is that this me-myself is not conscious. It is a mechanical action or construct, unconscious, habitual, and oblivious to all except itself. Thus, the third thing is that, when speaking of conscious placement of Attention, it is not possible for the me-myself (or the "our" of which Mister Lee speaks) to do anything consciously. Therefore, conscious placement of Attention must, by definition, arise from another source entirely, outside of the domain of me-myself. Instead, it is an act of the Being. This is a conscious action, and it is the only conscious action of which one is capable. It places the Being in the present reality, wherein the Being becomes subject to the will of God and ceases to act of its own will.

Thus, Mister Lee is exact in his discussion of placement of Attention. The Being places itself consciously in the field of surrender to the will of God; that is all it can do. Everything else is done by the will of God, including placement of Attention in the present. The Being makes its conscious move, and then it does not interfere with the will of God.

Awake? Or Asleep and Dreaming?

How can one possibly know for sure just *what* is a conscious move and *what* is a move made by the false, the me-myself? How can one be sure? Is there an objective measure by which one may know when one is conscious, awake, and in the present reality, and not just kidding oneself, dreaming, imagining, and falling once again into personal history?

Well, yes. One is provided with an objective measuring device by which one may gauge whether one is awake or asleep and dreaming. The body can serve as an objective mechanism to orient the Being in the present. It provides landmarks for this orientation:

1. *Erect posture*: Zen teaches that this posture alone is the awakened position; unconscious postures slouch, stoop, and use unnecessary tension; erect posture is yet another form of self remembering.

2. *Conscious placement of Attention down in the body, below the neck*: This move does not happen mechanically, but only from intention; ordinary attention is in the mind alone.

3. *Sense the breath*: Sensation is an objective phenomenon, always and only present, thus it cannot be faked or imagined; breath is real and observable; it can't be faked or imagined; it is a present phenomenon only.

4. *Sense the whole body*: The body is always and only present; it cannot be faked or imagined; bodily sensation orients the Being in the present, the now of the body. Many

people cannot sense the whole body at first; begin then with a limb or some part of the body which can be sensed.

5. *Relax the whole body:* This is a conscious process made from awareness of tension. If you find that you cannot relax, begin to work there, wherever you find yourself.

Now, I am completely in the body, fully embodied, present in the now of the body; otherwise, "I" is merely an idea, a recoil from reality, a figment of imagination.

From there, let it settle itself.

Therefore, in really studying this question via self observation, what I have observed is that when Attention is consciously located at the heart/abdominal region, Attention will gradually move to other centers as it is needed and wanted, depending upon what the action of the sacred descending energy requires.

Purification of Centers

Madame de Salzmann speaks elsewhere of the need for "purification" of the centers when entering into the union of the higher and the lower centers. In my own process, I am just now at exactly this point of purification of the centers. This purification is on many levels: physical, emotional, psychological, and spiritual. It is often physically painful. The emotional component is demanding and difficult, because there is no escaping the seeing of one's habitual emotional tendencies. The result is intense intentional suffering.

At the beginning of the last chapter I used a diagram of the enneagram provided by my friend Lee van Laer. You will notice that he indicates at the point sol-la in the enneagram the entrance of intentional suffering, followed immediately at the point si by purification. This is lawful. Once I seek to consciously unite the higher with the lower in me, the centers must be purified in order to accomplish this, by law. The energy knows what to do, so long as me-myself does not interfere. But I must bear the suffering that results, without complaint, or trying to change what is. As Arnaud Desjardins has taught, one learns to "accept what is, as it is, here and now." This is work, and work is hard. It demands that one remain positioned in the now of the body—present and with full Attention—and stay with whatever arises, neither suppressing nor expressing it, simply accepting without judgment. Take no position regarding the arising of phenomena.

What I am suggesting by pointing out the solar plexus region as a resting place or center of gravity for Attention is that this is a good beginning place, a sanctuary, for Attention to reside while this purification is underway. Why? Because the instinctive center at the navel, the sex center at the lower abdomen, and the heart center at the breast are contaminated by personal history and must be purified. What is most efficient during this process is to find a bodily location without contamination, from which one may observe more objectively what arises and is burned up by this purification process. To avoid constant identification with what arises, such a location at the abdominal region of the solar plexus is one possibility, because it is less contaminated by personal history. It is sanctuary for the Attention.

Sri Ramana Maharshi indicates this location, "between the two nipples [the body's midline. RH], below the chest and above the abdomen." This is roughly where the solar plexus is located. He then indicates that if one moves "two digits to the right is the heart." He is calling this the location of the "spiritual heart" which he says is the seat of the Self, and he continues, "all the psychic nerves depend upon it," which is much as Mister Gurdjieff suggests in his talk about the solar plexus in *Beelzebub's Tales to His*

Grandson (see quote below). Ramana Maharshi continues by saying that it is "the center of spiritual experience."

As the purification process is fully engaged, I have seen that the energy of Attention seeks its own level or center of gravity, without my interference, while I practice active passivity. Madame says, in the quote above, "I have to feel the necessity to change this relation so that my body and my functions accept a state of voluntary passivity." It is an active passivity, in which Attention is held in place, functions are observed without identification or movement either toward or away from the arising impressions, and one does not interfere with the movement of energy in the body. One keeps the body consciously relaxed. "I" remains passive, but actively vigilant, with conscious intention. This state of passivity is a feminine, or receptive, state. The feminine is awakened within and the feminine aspect of the Being emerges.

The creation of sanctuary, the active holding of Attention in place, is masculine force; the reception of Divine influence is feminine force: the marriage of the masculine and feminine forces within. For a long, long time, this is impossible. Only when Presence and Attention are developed and strengthened may one remain in place, consciously relaxed, and not identified with arising phenomena. In the meantime, there is the struggle to remain present.

The Guardian at the Gate

Energy is constantly being received from above, descending into the body through the top of the head. One must be alert and sensitive to sensation in order to verify this. Thus, one may wish to leave a guardian, a sensation-Attention, at the top of the head in order to monitor incoming energy impressions. This is vigilance, so that, as the impulse to thought arises, one may remain in place lower down in the body. What one may see, with patient observation over a period of time, is that this incoming energy enters as a pulsation and carries with it an entire, a holistic, impression which can be observed as a whole "knowing" all at once, not linearly, not step by step, as the mind operates. But then immediately, providing one stays in place at the abdominal region, one can observe the mind moving to capture this energetic impression and begin to unroll it in words and images, step by step—that which has already been seen in its entirety as a flash or pulsation of energetic impression.

The mind steals this energy unconsciously and mechanically in order to capture Attention for its own selfishly programmed aim: to restore and replay its stored patterns, the personal history. But by staying in place, this "capture and consume" process is short-circuited. It does not unfold. Instead, the energy continues to move with the breath. Impressions are energy, and the body transforms this energy into a finer energy, Being-food. Thus, I eat the impression. As I described this pattern repeatedly in my previous book, *Self Observation*, "Sometimes I eat the bear, sometimes the bear eats me."

Therefore, if I am able to remember myself and stay in place at the abdominal region, and do not move in identification with the seed-thought, there is no force in the mind to unscroll that energy in the form of linear thought. The mind cannot steal the incoming, descending energy-impression for its own selfish purposes. It cannot operate without my agreement by moving Attention upward, back into the mind so that it can replay its patterns. Therefore, the impulse of thought does not reach the will, does not impact the central nervous system. Attention remains free of identification and association.

A free Attention is able to observe objectively. If one can remain awake at this moment, the energy in the body is not stolen but moves downward, and then the body is able to transform it into a finer energy and move it back upward so the Being is fed; thus it develops and matures. In this way one becomes a food source for our Creator, by cooperating instead of interfering. One needs to stay fluid and vigilant here, not rigid. Attention will settle and adjust without effort. One just needs to remain relaxed and present. Be gentle and flexible.

Erect posture, the conscious placing of Attention at the solar plexus region, sensing the breath, sensing the whole body, and relaxing the whole body may be called first-stage self remembering, from which work may begin—the work of self observation without judgment (identification) or trying to change what is observed.

Gurdjieff's Instruction

Mister Gurdjieff has given the following to us regarding this bodily location at the solar plexus. In his first series (*Beelzebub's Tales to His Grandson*) he has this to say regarding this bodily location:

> *So in your favorites also there exists a corresponding localization for the concentration of all results issuing from the affirmation of the "head brain" and from all the shades of denial of the "spinal marrow"; and these results thereafter serve as a "regulating" or "reconciling principle" for the functioning of the whole presence of each of them.*
>
> *As regards the place of concentration of this localization, which serves the common presence of terrestrial three-brained beings as a "regulating" or "reconciling principle," it should be noted that in the beginning, in them as in us, this third concentration existed in your favorites in the form of* an independent brain *[my emphasis. RH], localized in the region of what is called the "breast."*

But after the process of their ordinary being-existence begAN to change markedly for the worse, Great Nature, due to certain causes flowing from the common-cosmic trogo-autoegocratic process, was compelled to change, without destroying its actual functioning, the system of localization of this brain of theirs.

That is to say, Great Nature gradually dispersed this organ, which had been concentrated in one place, into small localizations over their whole common presence, but chiefly in the region of what is called the "pit of the stomach." They themselves at the present time call the totality of these small localizations in this region the "solar plexus," or the "complex of nodes of the sympathetic nervous system. (713-714)

Try to intuit what Mister Gurdjieff is implying with this information. The region of the solar plexus or "breast" area once contained a center of energy transformation which served as a "reconciling force" or "neutralizing force" between two opposing forces, one from the "head brain" and one from the spine, thus transforming these combined energies into a third force. This center was, then, one of the chief centers of energy transformation in the body. And while these nerve nodes were at some point dispersed throughout the whole body, mainly they were localized in the solar plexus. That is, this brain-system for the transformation of two separate energies into higher Being-food is localized in the solar plexus.

But there is more. Mister Gurdjieff continues his explanation of the functioning of this center by speaking of the various functions of this transformed "Being-food." He tells us:

And so, like ourselves, the three-brained beings of the planet Earth are not only apparatuses . . . for transforming cosmic substances required for the Most Great Trogoautoegocrat [God. RH] but also have the possibility, while absorbing these substances coming from three independent sources, of assimilating, in addition to the substances indispensable for their own existence, certain substances destined for the coating and perfecting of their own higher being-bodies.

In this way those three-sourced substances entering their common presence for transformation are, for them just as for us, a threefold Being-food.

. . . The "second-sourced" substances . . . enter into them for further evolutionary transformation . . . as the "second Being-food," which is, as they say, the "air" they breathe; and it is these substances in the air that serve for the coating and maintenance of the existence of their "second being-body."

Finally, the substances of the "first source" which, for them as well as for us, are a third kind of Being-food [impressions. RH] serve for the coating and perfecting of the "highest being-body" itself.

When the abnormal conditions of ordinary being-existence were finally fixed there—with the result that both the instinctive and the intentional striving for self-perfecting disappeared from their essence—they not only ceased to feel the need to absorb these cosmic substances consciously, but even lost the knowledge and understanding of the existence and significance of "higher Being-foods." (714-716)

Step one

Mister Gurdjieff tells us some remarkable information regarding this first stage of self remembering: *erect posture, the conscious placement of Attention at the solar plexus, sensing the breath, sensing the body, and relaxing the body.*

The human biological instrument is a transformational instrument, when operated at its higher function. But it may only operate at this level with the conscious volition, intention, and cooperation of the inner Being. Mister E.J. Gold tells us that the pressure exerted by the continual placement of Attention on the body awakens it to this higher function (*Life in the Labyrinth*, 51).

At the mechanical level, the intellectual-emotional complex is constantly interfering with this process of transformation of energy into higher Being-food. But when the placement of Attention is done consciously, not only does this energy transformation feed higher entities, he informs us that it also serves to create "certain substances destined for the coating and perfecting of their own higher Being-bodies." When one works consciously, in harmony with our Creator, and does not interfere with the descending energy, this conscious labor acts in the service of creating a Being-body which may survive physical death. He tells us that the food for creating this body is air.

Thus, self remembering, the conscious placement of Attention at the solar plexus, and the conscious assimilation of air, "sensing the breath," are a conscious alignment with the forces of transformation both in the Ray of Creation and physically in the human body. Furthermore, he notes that the conscious assimilation of the third Being-food (see Chapter 9: *Completing the Inner Triad* for further discussion of Being-food), which is energetic impressions, serves to coat and perfect the "highest Being-body" or one which, on our level, we are told by Mister Gurdjieff is immortal in our solar system. But this happens only when the invocation of Presence and Attention are intensified by the methodical practice of invocation, via self remembering and self observation; that is, the struggle to remain present. When these two Being-aspects are developed to the degree that they can be invoked with steady and stable force, then the body becomes a fully functional, higher transformational instrument (E.J. Gold).

But Mister Gurdjieff relates that when certain necessary physiological changes became necessary in the human body, in order to maintain a cosmic balance, humans operating on a mechanical, unconscious level lost "the instinctive and the intentional striving for self-perfecting." Only the conscious practice of returning Attention to the now of the body, the present, can place one in alignment with this cosmic process. This striving for the perfection of the higher Being-bodies must be, lawfully, "instinctive and intentional" or it does not take place and one will live a mechanical life and die an unconscious, mechanical death.

The "conscious shock" of air and impressions requires that self remembering take place at the moment of receiving these two types of Being-food or their energy will serve only as a mechanical, unconscious force for the maintenance of the body on the survival level alone. William Patrick Patterson says,

> As we see with the musical scale, there comes a gap, a shock point, a Stopinder, as Gurdjieff calls it. Self-remembering has increased, however subtly, the quality of our vibration. Whatever the shock, we can absorb it if our vibrations, and the clarity that accompanies it, is equal to or greater than the shock. Life, in this sense, is really "eat or be eaten." Absorbing the shock, we assimilate its energy; we become more awake. Otherwise, we descend to a lower state in which our lives are nothing but the drama of walking a city of dream streets.
> —*Spiritual Survival*, 224.

If one's level of self remembering has reached the point where one is able to stay out of personal identification with the received impression shock, if one can stay in place with Attention lower down in the body, then the body knows what to do with the energy of the shock; it knows how to transform it into Being-food, with the result that I become more awake. I either eat the impression-shock, or it eats me—meaning it consumes my Attention.

However, what Mister Gurdjieff does not say here is just as important as what he does say. He suggests that the area of the breast/solar plexus was once an independent brain system whose nerve nodes were dispersed around the body, but mainly at the solar plexus. What he does not say, but what I intuit as a possibility, is that only by conscious labor may this region once again—possibly—be revitalized, reawakened, and re-enlivened to become a vital functioning force in the transformation of the Being. When Attention is consciously placed in this region, is it possible that a transformational force may be reactivated which is aligned with the laws of world creation and world maintenance? This is third-stage self remembering: I remember who I am, my place in the body, my place in the cosmic scale, and my relationship with our Creator. (See Chapter 9: *Completing the Inner Triad.*) To remain present without identification seems impossible without the help of our Creator, thus the need for conscious invocation of the help of the Divine in order to be present where the Divine is situated: in the here-now, the present.

By so doing, I make myself available to serve our Creator. But Mister Gurdjieff has more to say about locating Attention at the solar plexus in his third series, *Life Is Real Only Then, When I Am.* Here he gives an exercise which enlivens this latent independent brain system. His instruction for this exercise with the solar plexus is as follows:

For the correct understanding of the significance of this first assisting exercise it is first of all necessary to know that when a normal man, that is, a man who already has his real I, his will, and all the other properties of a real man, pronounces aloud or to himself the words "I am," then there always proceeds in him, in his, as it is called, "solar plexus," a so to say "reverberation," that is, something like a vibration, a feeling, or something of the sort.

This kind of reverberation can proceed also in other parts of his body in general, but only on the condition that, when pronouncing these words, his attention is intentionally concentrated on them.

If the ordinary man, not having as yet in himself data for the natural reverberation but knowing of the existence of this fact, will, with conscious striving for the formation in himself of the genuine data which should be in the common presence of a real man, correctly and frequently pronounce these same and for him as yet empty words, and will imagine that this same reverberation proceeds in him, he may thereby ultimately through frequent repetition gradually acquire in himself a so to say theoretical "beginning" for the possibility of a real practical forming in himself of these data.

He who is exercising himself with this must at the beginning, when pronouncing the words "I am," imagine that this same reverberation is already proceeding in his solar plexus.

Here, by the way, it is curious to notice that as a result of the intentional concentration of this reverberation on any part of his body, a man can stop any disharmony which has arisen in this said part of the body, that is to say, he can for example cure his headache by concentrating the reverberation on that part of the head where he has the sensation of pain.

At the beginning it is necessary to pronounce the words "I am" very often and to try always not to forget to have the said reverberation in one's solar plexus.

Without this even if only imagined experiencing of the reverberation, the pronouncing aloud or to oneself of the words "I am" will have no significance at all . . .

First of all, concentrate the greater part of your attention on the words themselves, "I am," and the lesser part concentrate on the solar plexus, and the reverberation should gradually proceed of itself. (134-135)

I will add to this my own experience with this exercise, over the course of nearly three years. When I do this practice, which is several times during my sitting, and then again at quiet moments, and during the course of the day when I pray or remember myself, I include with this sensation an awareness of the external environment (second stage), and of God/guru (third stage). I issue the "I am" phrase not from the mind, but sense it directly from the solar plexus, often on the inhalation, but not always. Almost from the start, I sensed this "reverberation" which Mister Gurdjieff speaks of, very intensely and often throughout my entire nervous system, from head to toe. Sometimes I feel nothing, of course, at which moments I do as he said, I imagine this sensation. Sometimes the reverberation is so intense that the entire body vibrates. At other times, an immense joy arises from the solar plexus area. Still at other times, I have experienced a deep Being-laughter, a laugh of joy rising up from this solar plexus area. This is why I say that perhaps it is possible to reawaken and enliven this "independent brain."

This is a kind of self remembering of another order, a third stage. What I know from my own experience is that there is a definite, observable, vibratory effect throughout the entire central nervous system when doing this exercise regularly, as indicated. Sometimes the effect in me is to deeply move me to tears of gratitude. I do not pretend to understand all that this accomplishes.

What is important to note is that, with this stage of self remembering, associated with self observation, I may avoid the error which Mister A. R. Orage made in his work with Mister Gurdjieff, and which Mister Gurdjieff himself describes in *Life Is Real. . .* in this way:

> *Mr. Orage . . . managed with only the primary information, out of the whole totality of information throwing light on all my ideas, which concerned that question about which I spoke in the last lecture, that is to say, the question of so-called "self observation," namely . . . the knowledge of which is indeed quite indispensable at the beginning for everyone who is striving to learn the truth, but which, if it becomes the center of gravity for the mentation of man, will . . . unfailingly lead to just the result which, to my great regret, I observe now in almost every one of you.* (96)

It appears that Orage's error was to focus on the practice of self observation exclusively, without its accompanying practice of self remembering, as well as the totality of the teaching and its ideas. Likewise, Robert Burton (a Fourth Way teacher) focused exclusively on self remembering, without its accompanying practice of self observation. It is not enough to *do* such an exercise. To merely do the exercise is to miss, to misunderstand, what is being called for here. In order for the practice to become transformational, one must "BE the practice." One must *become* the practice, so deeply integrated in Being that it becomes one's nature.

The only way that one can expand Attention to include self, other and God is by *sensing* this practice, not *thinking* one's way into this practice, although at first that is the only way one may attempt it. It is too much for the formatory brain to comprehend. But as this split Attention is practiced, slowly, slowly one begins to sense self remembering by sensation alone. The "I" becomes simply sensation-Attention. "I" becomes the practice. The Being relaxes into it as its essential nature. It becomes simply sensation-Attention sensed with the whole body, not with the mind alone. As a result of long and patient practice, one may have the experience of the whole body becoming a sense organ for Attention. Impressions are taken in not with the mind alone, but with the whole body as a sense organ. Relaxed body is *honest body*,* as Trungpa Rinpoche calls it. Try to intuit what this means without thinking about it.

This practice places me experientially in "Just This" (Mister Lee), experiencing what is, as it is, here and now (Arnaud Desjardins). "I" fully inhabits the entire body; thus, it becomes my experience, not a theory or an idea. It places me in organic ignorance (Da Free John) and "Organic Innocence" (Mister Lee)—in "I don't know." Try to intuit the difference between "knowing" and "experiencing." Trust the breath. It is always reliable and consistent. Follow the breath, sense the breath, stay with the breath, find the breath and stay with it. It is always and only a present phenomenon—thus, if I wish to work I must do so in the present: "It is only by working to be present that my attention will develop." (Madame de Salzmann. *The Reality of Being*, 30.)

The Disclaimer

Self observation alone is not enough. It must be brought down, out of the head-brain and into the body. Otherwise I kid myself, I imagine that I work, and my observation is not grounded and anchored in the body. Therefore I may become so self-absorbed, so self-centered, that my ordinary madness becomes quite unmanageable and out of control. That is why a group is necessary, as a reliable feedback mechanism.

What is even more preferable is that I work under the guidance of a spiritual master and in a sangha of work practitioners gathered around that master. This is how I have worked and it has saved me, a liar and a hopeless idiot, from countless, but not all serious, errors—especially the imaginary error that me-myself knows something and has some kind of so-called certainty about the Work.

The only thing I am certain of is my own personal experience and my wish to work. There will be errors in a book like this, brought about by my own predilections and eccentricities. Therefore, you must *verify!* for yourself. Self observation is a self-correcting mechanism. It will guide you until conscience awakens, at which point you will have an utterly reliable guide for your inner growth and maturity.

As I have said, this chapter is tricky, because I don't know anything. I only have my own experience to guide me, so my experience with placement of Attention at the solar plexus has been rewarding, but it could just as well be the big toe (as a certain dear nameless Joker once suggested). So this chapter is the result of research, experience, and intuition.

Finally, in his first series (*Beelzebub*), Mister Gurdjieff explains that the solar plexus was once an independent brain system. Then in his third series (*Life Is Real*) he leaves us with the "I am" exercise, and he places "I am" at the solar plexus. "I am" is the Being, so this is an exercise to develop the inner Being. Not only that, but he then titles this third series *Life Is Real Only Then, When I Am.* Only when "I am" awakens to itself, remembers itself, does life become real—and he locates "I am" at the solar plexus.

I do not wish to convince you of anything here, nor am I pushing for one location of Attention over another, because that is obviously a false note, as the quotes from many realized Masters indicate. I am merely honestly and openly detailing my own thought process, in order to arrive at the solar plexus as one possible starting point for the investigation.

From there, let it settle itself.

You must explore for yourself, and see for yourself what results you find. You can't make my, or anyone else's, experience yours. Lord have mercy on us and on our investigations; I wish to work.

I will leave you with this interesting quote from Chris Griscom (author and psychic healer):

Anxiety is expressed visually when we cross our arms over our chest or solar plexus. By doing this we try to protect ourselves emotionally from some threat. This starts when we receive vibrations from our surroundings via the solar plexus at a very young age.

When the vibrations around us are negative, as a result of anger, self-righteousness, or anxiety, we as children automatically become tense in the solar plexus chakra because the emotional body is imprinted by outside vibrations through this center. The tension is a result of the fact that those vibrations do not correspond to the child's naturally higher vibrations. That which normally evokes a fight-or-flight response is absorbed and repressed—in other words, no longer consciously perceived in the course of time. We nonetheless continue to register the vibrations surrounding us through the emotional body. The result is that we bend over at the stomach to a greater or lesser extent, and we attempt to protect the solar plexus by covering it with our arms. The gesture that is supposed to afford us protection, however, has the opposite effect. The solar plexus center atrophies as we no longer permit it to work in its natural way, that is by emitting energy of its own.

In our physical body we generally carry our anxiety across the breadth of our chest . . . Everything that partially or wholly blocks our breathing, such as smoking, sources or enhances anxiety. A sure sign of anxiety is tension in the shoulders . . . Anxiety is expressed visually when we cross our arms over our chest or solar plexus. By doing this we try to protect ourselves emotionally from some threat.

—*The Healing of Emotion: Awakening the Fearless Self,*
23-24.

From there, let it settle itself.

I told the doctor I was overtired, anxiety ridden, compulsively active, constantly depressed, with recurring fits of paranoia. Turns out I'm normal.

—Jules Feiffer

Stacking the Woodpile

I am stacking a chord of split logs against
the coming winter. I sort them in 3 groups to begin;
the flat pieces are for leveling the pile, placed
under larger logs to even out a row, one row stacked
end to end, the next side by side for a stable pile;
the short stubby triangular pieces are filler,
great to fill in gaps or at either end of a row
where wood meets iron posts which hold up the carport;

then there are the big heavy logs which anchor the pile,
make its foundation, and stabilize the rows.
I think of the Anasazi stone masons whose similar style
made stone walls that stood 1,000 years and those
walls tell you about the men who built them: without guile,
careful, in love with detail, mindful; only God knows
their names, their bodies are dust, the walls alone still stand;
into the valley of death they bring an ordered mind, a careful hand.

Red Hawk

CHAPTER 11

The Holy Present and the 1-Percent Edge

Throughout the weekend of [Aikido] Spring Camp we were reminded to remain externally relaxed and receptive and internally strong and unified . . . This is a profound energetic shift, a re-organizing of the habit body . . . What if we were to place our attention on sensations as they arose or even after they have arisen and just hold steady, right there, relaxing into the stillness, feeling without placing our attention on the opposing force . . . the desire to open up the orgasmic relief valve . . . ahhhhh! What if we just stayed with the feeling and waited?
—Lesley Ball. *Tawagoto* 19:2 (Summer 2006), 162.

The characteristic of this second state, of self-remembering, is divided attention . . . First, for certain cosmic reasons, no one can attempt it or practise it until he is first told about it and it is explained to him . . . But this self-remembering can not be repeated or maintained except by his conscious effort. It can not happen of itself. It can never become a habit. And the moment the idea of self-remembering or divided attention is forgotten, all efforts, no matter how sincere, degenerate once again into "fascination", that is, into awareness of one thing at a time . . . Thus it is necessary to point out that close attention put into a task, into physical awareness of one's body, into mental exercises of one sort or another . . . does not of itself constitute self-remembering. For all this may be done with undivided attention, that is, one may become "fascinated" by a task, by physical awareness . . . Thus self-remembering, or the practice of divided attention—though the first glimpse of it may seem extraordinarily simple, easy and obvious—in reality requires a complete reconstruction of one's whole life and point of view, both towards oneself and other people. As long as one believes that one can alter oneself, or alter other people; as long as one believes that one has the power to do, that is, to make things other than they are, either internally or externally, the state of self-remembering seems to retreat from one the more efforts one makes to achieve it.

—Rodney Collin, 235.

Built into the human biological instrument, hardwired into the central nervous system, is a kind of attention which is automatic, mechanical, and unconscious. It is required for the survival of the organism in nature. I may drive from home to my office, let us say, and when I arrive at the office I cannot tell you a single thing I saw, what happened on the way, or how I arrived safely. But I did arrive alive and this is how that level of attention operates. There is complete unconsciousness, like a coma, an automatic pilot, and that is the level most people operate at most of the time. I survive, but I cannot tell you how.

Nature programs for survival. This is living in survival mode. It is completely selfish, self-oriented, self-only level of survival. It is not about relationship. The danger of a book like this, which speaks directly of the Work, is that this information will simply become more useless data stored in the mechanical part of the intellect and memorized so one may speak mechanically about ideas with which one has no practical knowledge based on struggle, suffering, and personal experience. This is not a book to be read; it is a manual to be studied and worked with, then put down while one goes into the struggle. Then one gains practical knowledge which may be applied to the practices described here. It may be useful to intuit this quote from Chögyam Trungpa Rinpoche:

> *There is no hope of understanding anything at all. There is no hope of finding out who did what or what did what or how anything worked. Give up your ambition to put the jigsaw puzzle together. Give it up altogether, absolutely; throw it up in the air, put it in the fireplace. Unless we give up this hope, this precious hope, there is no way out at all.*
> —*Crazy Wisdom*, 84.

The Holy Present

The practice of self remembering/self observation requires another level of Attention entirely; it requires the awakening of the second Attention, a conscious Attention. This places one on a different level, inside, from ordinary humanity. It aligns one with "Organic Ignorance," with "I don't know mind," which Chögyam Trungpa suggests is "the way out." Self remembering calls for a conscious shift within, bringing Attention below the neck and finding its place, its home, so to speak, its center of gravity, in the body. This is called "return to the Mother" by Lao Tsu and others.

When I consciously align my posture, place Attention in the abdominal area of the solar plexus/heart chakra, sense the breath, sense the body, and relax the body, I am "in place" and able to observe myself in a new way. I can see more from this bodily location than I ever could from the mind alone. I see my own ignorance. This conscious shift of Attention is what is known as "awakening the second Attention," or in the Shamanic traditions, "shifting the assemblage point." And when Attention is in place, "I am." With Attention at the solar plexus region, I can observe the movements of mind and emotion, without moving toward or away from them in identification, which is what Lesley is suggesting is possible in the quote above.

What this conscious placement of Attention does is to place the Being in the holy present, the here-now, the now of the body. The present is the great mystery, the realm of the miraculous which Mister Ouspensky was "in search of." In the present, all personal history is erased; there is only what is, as it is, here and now. The constant, self-referencing me-myself is passive and quiet. In the present, it cannot gain a foothold. Suddenly I am free to be.

God is a present-phenomenon only. It is a living force which manifests in this reality as non-judgmental love. All living things exist in only one place: the present. Nothing is alive in the past, in the mind, in thought. Nothing is alive in the future, which is merely the mind projecting the past in imagination. All possibility exists only in the present. The conscious movement of Attention into the present is prayer. It is the invitation to surrender. It brings one at once into direct experience rather than living at secondhand, through the mind as filter. This move invites relationship; it joins one with the immediate environment and with others. This movement into the unknown involves giving up the hope that understanding alone can free me.

Avoiding Relationship

The exact nature of this me-myself (or ego) with which I have identified most of my life is worth recapitulating here. Me-myself is a lie, an imaginative creation, an intellectual conceit, a collection of memories which coalesce around a central organizing principle which the Work calls "chief feature," and which I am calling "the blind spot." This me-myself is not an entity, it is an action. It is the strategy to avoid relationship, an act of recoil from the present, where love resides. Thus, me-myself is the very action of avoiding love; it is the active betrayal of love by turning one's back upon God.

Self remembering, on the other hand, is the bodily worship of the Divine; it is the alignment with the living Divine love-current constantly descending into the human body. Therefore, me-myself is the recoil into fear. It is, in fact, fear itself. It is a fear-based mechanism to avoid relationship. It is the state of ordinary humanity, characterized chiefly by two things: identification and distraction. One might even say that the life of an ordinary human is composed almost entirely of distractions and the identification with these distractions (witness the universal numbing and deadening addiction to technology).

Real Love Must Find Me

Self remembering and self observation do not change the inner world, they change my relationship to it. What is more, they give birth to an entirely new state of consciousness, an expanded state in which I come alive to my life and my Attention expands ever so slowly, without force or violence, to include more and more life. It is this expansion of Attention which opens the gate to the present and creates for the first time the possibility that real love can find me. This simple gesture, done repeatedly and intentionally without violence, develops patience, fortitude and perseverance. Transformation is homeopathic, in small incremental shifts and gradually awakening Awareness. It is beautiful, kind and methodical. It is practical work.

> *The idea of work is that consciousness can untie all the knots. So as an act of faith you try to confront yourself, try to come towards yourself, not violently, because then you rebound from that door. Maybe if you come quietly toward that door and try many, many times, maybe it will spring open.*
>
> —Lord John Pentland

One may no longer be aware of the person one was before this practice began, because one is no longer that person. Now, one is sometimes conscious, where before one was unconscious. One might even say that now there are moments where "I am," when before I was not. There was simply no one here except a fabrication calling itself "me-myself," merely an idea, a recoil. Now there is Presence and Attention. This Presence is a shift in context. Presence exists in the present and returns again and again to the present because that is its home. This joining, this merging into love, allows the Being to emerge from its cocoon.

> *I need to know this Presence as something really existing . . . I can come to it if I am actively passive, quiet enough for an energy of another quality to appear, to be contained in me. This is a state of deep letting go where the functions are maintained in passivity. I let my functions come into my Presence. I do not go into them; they come into me. Only the attention is active, an attention coming from all the centers.*
>
> —Jeanne de Salzmann, *The Reality of Being*, 82.

The destination is the present—it must be constantly renewed with every breath or the connection is lost.

The 1-Percent Edge

The conscious placement of Attention down lower in the body, in the area of the solar plexus, places Attention where I may get an objective view of the movements of each of these centers and have the chance, the possibility, of not being taken in identification. When this simple gesture is done consistently, beginning again moment to moment, there is a gradual gentle shift within.

As one is now, one exists as me-myself, an unconscious, habitual, fear-based mechanism. This mechanism has the final say in life, even though there exists in all of us an innate basic goodness (Chögyam Trungpa) which sometimes prevails, but is quickly and easily overruled by me-myself. However, years of patient inner work have produced in me a remarkable, one might even say miraculous, shift: it has given the Work a 1-percent edge over me-myself. That is, the ego is still active, demanding, voracious, and hugely resistant to any form of work. Nevertheless, it no longer has final authority. Though it often captures Attention and old habits prevail, they do not prevail for long, nor so often, and when they do, the urgency of conscience impels me to either forgive or apologize as quickly as possible—which has become very quickly over the years. Yet apology can become automatic and habitual. Without genuine feeling it can become uncaring. So beware!

In other words, years of patient work have given the Work (the Being) 51 percent say within. The me-myself, that inner "F---you, eat cookies, watch movies, sleep late" life-form, still has 49-percent command authority, but the majority vote is the slim, but absolutely crucial, 1-percent majority: 51 percent to 49 percent.

The work-edge, the 1-percent edge, contains all the possibilities for transformation and alignment with the will of God. It is this 1-percent edge which the Work offers and which contains reality, real life, and the possibility of love. My experience is that in order to gain this 1-percent edge, enormous sacrifice is required; one must pay. And what one has to pay with is one's suffering. And oh, how me-myself loves and clings to its suffering, its drama. The conscious placement of Attention in the present is a move to sacrifice one's suffering, and lay it as an offering at the feet of God, as prasad. What could be finer than to enter fully into one's own life and live it fully? To be present is to be alive. Then, and only then, is real friendship possible. One works with more and more understanding, becoming ever more aware of one's inner depth and mystery. One works with understanding and Attention, working with what is uncovered, working *for* more Presence. Now, for the first time, there is a real aim in life: to be more present. This creates a spark of life which grows each time one breathes on it. I remember: Ah, I am present, I know where I am and what my purpose is; finally, life has meaning. To be present is to be what love is.

True Nature Emerging

This is how our true nature emerges: non-judgmental love is Being-nature. Self remembering and self observation gradually consume everything which is not true nature; basic goodness emerges from the chaos of fear-based me-myself.

Why do I mistakenly think it is so important to entertain the thought or emotion? Because I am identified with the process of thought and emotion, so I cling to the process. However, what is crucial to evolution is that I *see* and *feel* the process, how it takes me away from the present, and then easefully and gently, without reaction or judgment, return to the present. Allow the process itself, regardless of content, to be dissolved, consumed, and digested. One eats the me-myself.

This relationship to the process differs from repression. Repression is identification: I am that which I observe—I judge it, then I fight to suppress or change it; I force the issue, tension results, and I am lost; I disappear and me-myself emerges. Then there is only self and no other, no Awareness of my surroundings; there is no love, only fear and the resulting tension.

Once I have discovered the present for myself, I have discovered the doorway to freedom. To be present is to be free of the past, which is fear. I have discovered the open secret, which few know or understand, or want to know. I have found where our Creator has hidden itself, out in the open where few think to look. In fact, when I think, I cannot look anywhere except at shadows on a cave wall. I turn inward, turn my back upon the wide open present. Once present, the function of self observation is to consume all illusions including, and especially, me-myself, which is the great and only illusion. Every inner movement— every thought, every emotion, every reaction—and every action is this illusory me-myself. Every inner movement is this illusion, except the conscious placement of Attention, which is a Being-movement and is conscious, not mechanical.

Do not be fooled by this book into believing it explains self remembering. A book cannot do that. There are as many different explanations of the practice as there are people doing it. Stop thinking about the practice and simply be. If I am thinking about practice, I am not present. These steps and stages are so obvious and simple . . ., but not necessarily easy. And one final note of warning: what is described in this book is a technology for inner Work. The great danger, the trap, is that I become identified with the technology and lose sight of the purpose for it. I foolishly try to build my home on the map instead of building my home on the actual ground on which I walk and live my life. The technology is a means for observing what has caught and held Attention; it is not a means to divert or distract Attention from seeing where energy is moving in the body.

I cannot remember myself because it requires consciousness to do so, and in me consciousness is not developed. Thus I do not have the means to remain present for more than a second or two. I have to develop Attention and Presence by struggling to remain present. I have to see that I am helpless before my addictions and habits. I have to suffer this seeing and feeling for a very long time. Slowly, slowly consciousness develops, grows, and matures in me. It is a natural process and natural processes take time; the acorn does not become an oak tree quickly.

The Stillness of Love

The present is where love dwells; it is real and true. To be present is to be real. One grows quiet when one is present. When in the company of others, I may be agreeable, social, polite, considerate, but most of all, when I am present I am attentive. I listen deeply, interrupt seldom, complain rarely, and I respond to others. This active listening brings others out more and invokes something real in them as well. It is a law: Presence invokes Presence. The law of conscious love is this: non-judgmental love elicits the same in the other. I love, therefore I am.

Thus, relationship becomes deeper, more intimate, even though I do not speak as much. Conscious listening, allowing gaps of silence to develop, following what others are saying and responding, giving others one's full Attention; these are all acts of conscious love. Non-judgmental love is present-Attention.

Present-Attention builds the 1-percent edge. The center of gravity of the self undergoes a shift in context when one consciously practices this realignment of Attention. One becomes more objective, impersonal, more selfless.

> *And in maintaining this alignment moment to moment, [we] enter into what we call Conscious surrender, which, in other words, is the active participation, with awareness and agreement . . . in the process, thereby, in Work terms, sharing the burden . . . of the Absolute, one of the sole reasons (only one, there are others) for our existence. So we can move from being surrendered because the Universe is entirely Itself . . . trying to swim against a current that it is impossible to swim against . . . move from this* [mechanical, unconscious— RH] *surrender, that is given "from above" or from "outside" so to speak . . . to a surrender that is one of a conscious acceptance of "what is, as it is, here and now", a "Yes" in place of the ever-constant "no" of ego. We cannot know the place of love and gratitude that Conscious Surrender avails us, disposes us to until this Conscious Surrender is true of us but if you need encouragement (there is no <u>proof</u> but the experience, the <u>abiding</u> experience itself) allow the testimonies of the saints and sages, mystics and Masters, of all the traditions and down and up through the ages to be of some value in helping you come to a conviction powerful enough to actually inspire you to practice with some degree of reliability and consistency, tenacity and faith.*
>
> —Lee Lozowick, *Chasing Your Tail*, 51-52.

The practice of realigning the Being is an alignment with surrender to the will of God and with the descending Divine love current. So this begins "the dance with God," in earnest, in which I constantly begin again, being sucked back into the mind, remembering myself and gently, gracefully, kindly bringing Attention back into alignment, back into the present, without judgment or drama. Over and over again, for years, thousands of times, without judgment.

The Inner Marriage

When Attention is brought to the region of the heart/solar plexus, the middle ground, then two different energies, two levels, meet and join there. The descending force and the ascending force meet and join. One may also say that here the masculine and the feminine are united within, to form a perfect marriage. The conscious placement of Attention, moving from mind to heart/solar plexus region, is a masculine force. The masculine creates sanctuary there by holding Attention and renewing it so that the feminine may safely emerge and passively, vulnerably, receive the guru and the will of God.

When this marriage within takes place, then my external relationships cease to be dependent or needy. I stand whole, a union within, and do not need to look for another person or circumstance outside me in order to be made whole. Only then may I join with another responsibly, reliably, consistently, in full and complete commitment and without dependency. Only then may I stand by my word and by those vows made to our Creator in matrimony. I can be trusted and have the inner courage to enter into a "No Exit" relationship in which, no matter what happens, we will work it out. Such a relationship stands upon the Work. All faith and hope are in the Work. In the Work I place my trust, relying upon it to show me the way. A relationship built upon this rock will not fail.

The mind is only the illusion of self. It has no other function ... All kinds of illusions may arise ... all kinds of experiences that lead you to think and act strangely and to assume that these experiences are signs of profound Realization. All visions and experiences must be transcended, every last one of them ... You must transcend all forms of experience that arise or you will go mad.

That is why one needs a guide, a Spiritual Master, to counter the torment and free one from illusion ... (81)

The process is a matter of whole bodily surrender of attention. It is a matter of being attention bodily, rather than being attention abstractly ... To practice this Way requires us to transcend abstract attention and to live in Divine Ignorance, to practice the Way as the bodily sacrifice of attention ... (198)

True self-observation takes place in Divine Ignorance, or whole bodily surrender in the context of Happiness, or in the Divine Being, the Radiant Divine, or Transcendental Person. Self-watching is something we do when we are contracted upon ourselves, when we are isolated as consciousness, when attention is a mental abstraction rather than a whole bodily process. (201)

—Da Free John, *The Bodily Location of Happiness.*

The Aims of the Work

The aims of the Work are three-fold (this may be gross over-simplification):

1. To create the 1-percent edge. All the practices and exercises, including self remembering and self observation, are to slowly build a work-body which eventually is

strong enough to create a 1-percent advantage within. In that case, the Being has the inner force to work *with* the powerful denying force, the resistance to work, which grows apace. Thus, the Being—which has the 1-percent edge—becomes the active principle, and the denying force becomes the passive principle. They work together.

2. The 1-percent edge allows the Being just enough force to find the present and begin the struggle to remain present, working with the denying force to find a stable inner alignment. The 1-percent edge allows the Being to find the open gate, the doorway to the Divine, which is the present. It allows the Being to place itself bodily in the position to be surrendered. It lays itself down in whole-body surrender at the feet of the Divine guru, whose sole domain is the present. The 1-percent edge allows the Being to function in "organic ignorance" (Da Free John), confessing, "I don't know." This is the great Being-confession, which transcends the mind's illusion, the lie that it knows. This confession transcends the enslavement, fascination and enthrallment with thought. Furthermore, it allows the Being to live as "organic inno- cence" (Lee Lozowick), which is a whole-body relaxation into the present, beyond fear.

3. Self remembering and self observation, the foundation practices of the Work, are meant to reveal the true nature of the mind. "The mind is only the illusion of self. It has no other function" (Da Free John). The mind is incapable of dealing with this statement, so it automatically rejects it. This must be grasped intuitively, as a whole-body shock of recognition and understanding, the bodily sensation of one's nothingness. It is the shock of Being-recognition. It

brings everything to rest. Years and years of practice bring one, eventually, to realization of one's nothingness. At this point, Being becomes Presence, and Attention is whole body, relaxed body, soft body, "honest body" (Chögyam Trungpa): whole-body-sensation Attention. The Being issues the invitation and waits silently in the present to receive the Divine current of non-judgmental love as it descends into the body at the top of the head. Then the Being becomes clear-light awareness.

Waiting for God

The Work brings the Being to the open doorway to the Divine, which is the present. There the Being waits with faith and patience to serve, to be of use. The Being can only stand in the doorway and wait to be taken in whole-bodily surrender. It can do no more. It has done its part. The rest— transcendence and transformation—is the work of the guru, the Divine-embodiment.

Herein lies the great secret of the Work: to create a 1-percent advantage for itself by conscious labor and intentional suffering, and thereby give the Being the inner force to voluntarily place itself at the feet of the Sacred Heart of Mercy, the bodily worship of the Divine:

1. Erect posture.
2. Conscious placement of Attention at the heart/solar plexus region.
3. Sense the breath.
4. Sense the whole body.
5. Relax the body.
6. Observe–Begin again. And again.

This point in the book is another excellent STOP! point—not to continue until you have practiced what is given here, collected material and questions to be shared with a group, and verified for yourself by your own personal experience the help and truth of what is being suggested here. It is through direct personal experience that I avoid the trap of believing that the technology is the end result instead of the means to an end. In the end, I wish to know myself. It is vital to see for oneself what results come from such practice—not because some so-called expert who has written a book says so. Any fool can write a book. *The destination is the present—it must be constantly renewed with every breath or the connection is lost.*

If you talk to God, you are praying; if God talks to you, you have schizophrenia.

—Thomas Szasz

Amo Ergo Sum

Descartes said, Cogito ergo sum;
I think, therefore I am.
He had it all wrong, of course, he
was an intellectual. I-Am,
is a statement of Being.
Being is not thinking.

Love is Being.
I love, therefore I Am.
To think about love
is not love, in the same way
that thinking about fire
will neither cook your food, nor
warm you on a winter night.
Love is fire; it brings heat and light.

Red Hawk

CHAPTER 12

The Law of Reciprocal Maintenance: Conscious Management of the Survival Instinct

One of the chief things which is taught in schools of the fourth way is intentional division of attention between oneself and the outside world. By long practice and constant exercise of will, the fine matter of awareness is not allowed to flow uninterruptedly in one direction, but is divided, one part being retained in oneself, while the other is directed outward towards whatever one may be studying or doing. By dividing attention, the student learns to be aware of himself speaking to another, of himself standing in a certain scene, of "himself" acting, feeling or thinking in relation to the outside world ... In this way he learns to remember himself, by moments at first, and then with increasing frequency. And in proportion as he learns to remember himself, so his actions acquire a meaning and consistency, which were impossible to them as long as his awareness moved only from one fascination to another.

The characteristic of this second state, of self-remembering, is divided attention. There are several strange things about this state. First, for certain cosmic reasons, no one can attempt it or practise it until he is first told about it and it is explained to him. Second, when it is explained to him, every normal person has enough will and energy to catch a momentary glimpse of what it means. If he wishes, he can in the moment that he hears about it, become aware of himself in his surroundings—of himself, sitting in a chair, reading about a new idea.

But this self-remembering cannot be repeated or maintained except by his conscious effort. It cannot happen of itself. It can never become a habit. And the moment the idea of self-remembering or divided attention is forgotten, all efforts, no matter how sincere, degenerate once again into "fascination", that is, into awareness of one thing at a time.

—Rodney Collin, 234-235.

Humans are created to provide a conscious link, an energy transformation instrument, between the Higher and the Earth. It does not take great numbers of humans to perform this task if they are capable of conscious labor. However, this is not the case with the mass of humanity. With the great mass of humanity on the Earth, because we have been granted by grace the freedom to choose whom we serve, most of us serve our own self importance, or egoic desires. We do not serve our Creator in a way which is useful for Its larger purposes of "world creation and world maintenance" (Mister Gurdjieff's terminology).

We are told that the "Luciferian rebellion" was a bloodless revolution, a revolution in philosophy. Lucifer had a difference in philosophy with God. His argument was that the angelic race was born to serve and it did so without question. However, Lucifer had a question. He questioned the justice of being made to serve automatically, without a choice, or without "free will." He felt that it was only just that the angelic beings have a choice in the matter. He lost his argument and he and his legions of followers, as the story goes, were cast out of Paradise: *Paradise Lost* (John Milton's great epic poem). The irony of this loss is that Lucifer and his minions gained what they wished for: free will. The Luciferian statement (or, one might say, Lucifer's rebellion) is, "I will not serve." This is the human condition and the human predicament. We angelic beings are born into a human biological instrument, which by its very nature is mammal, and here we refuse to serve the Higher. I choose to do things "my way." (See also: Red Hawk. *Raven's Paradise.* Treadwell, NY: Bright Hill Press. 2010, for an answer to Milton's *Paradise Lost.*)

Two Levels of Human Life

This mammal instrument may operate on two levels. The first is unconsciously, a level of mechanical, conditioned action-reaction, according to habits placed into it at our earliest childhood and carried out in endless repetition for the rest of the life of the body on Earth, or according to instinctive functions hardwired into the central nervous system. The result of such unconscious life is that the Being-within does not grow or mature, but remains fixed on an unconscious level, doomed to repeat in another body the same body of habits which was formed in it long ago.

However, there is a possibility for operation of this biological mammalian instrument on another level completely, a conscious level. But to activate this level of consciousness requires that the Being-within awaken to itself, begin to remember itself (which develops Presence); and by self observation (which develops Attention), which is a self-correcting mechanism built into the human body, we gain the capacity to grow and mature. The nature of this activity, known as the Work, requires both conscious labor—which is why it is called "work"—and intentional suffering. That is why so few are willing to undertake the lifelong struggle to awaken and to align themselves with the will of our Creator. "*I would rather do it my way, by myself, without interference or demand placed upon me.*" "*I prefer to remain mechanical and lazy.*" "*I will not serve.*" Thus my entire life on Earth is composed almost exclusively of distractions; that is, with mechanical recoil into fear and away from the present, which is Divine love, non-judgmental love. What I call "myself" is merely a recoil into fear, a separation from the Divine will which is found in the present, the here-now of the body.

In order to activate the awakening process within, I must find help and be taught what to do and how to do it. So this alone narrows the field of applicants for the Work, because I resist asking for help. Something has formed in me—I may call it "ego" or "myself"—which wants to do everything its own way and will not admit to the need for help. It refuses to see that it does not know, but remains forever in recoil, in the thrall of the illusion of knowing. It takes a great shock for the Being to be startled awake momentarily, enough to recognize that it does not know what it is doing and has never known. Such a shock leads me to seek help from one who does know what to do and how to do it. Only then is the process of self remembering and self observation active.

A Greater Relationship

For a long time, all of my efforts are directed toward freeing myself of the stranglehold which the intellectual-emotional complex has over my behavior. I wish to change what I see in me and I struggle for myself alone. Only after long struggle of this sort do I see that I have gained nothing and am going nowhere in this struggle. My intention is in the wrong direction and leads me only in a circle of repetition. Finally, I begin to enlarge the circle of my enquiry to include work with others, which produces a new level of suffering and a new source of shocks.

Thus, slowly, slowly, it begins to dawn on me that I do not work for myself alone, but for something so large that it cannot be named. "The Tao that can be told is not the eternal Tao.//The name that can be named is not the eternal name" (Lao Tsu. *Tao Te Ching*, One). Gradually I come to realize, intuitively, that I cannot act by myself, but only at the mercy of the Great Holy which cannot be named but whose mercy guides and directs all movement everywhere. I enter into the humbling process in which self-importance is broken open and broken down so that I may serve, voluntarily: "Lord have mercy; I wish to work."

Only then am I willing to make conscious sacrifice for the good of others and not for myself alone. Only then do I wish to work for the good of our Creator regardless of the cost to myself. This is the level of a mature Being who has seen and come to know oneself via self remembering and self observation. From long and patient self observation without judgment or trying to change what is observed, I begin to see what it is in me which prevents my serving as a lawful energy-transformer and feeding-mechanism in the service of our Creator (please see Chapter 9 for a discussion of energy as food, and what is required in me to allow this process to go forward). I observe what prevents me from aligning myself with the "law of reciprocal maintenance" (what is above maintains what is below, and what is below may reciprocate provided it does so consciously), which is how I may pay for my existence.

Life at the Survival Level

On the other hand, if I live as the mass of humanity lives in the outer world, I remain unconscious and I live at the creature level all of my life; that is, I live as a mammal in a mammal's body and I do as all mammals do. I behave as all two-brained creatures behave, as a creature living on the level of survival. This level is a recoil into fear, from which ego arises. Ego is a recoil from Divine love, from the will of our Creator. Ego is a refusal to serve. Life at the creature level is about one thing only: survival. Survival is always and only selfish. It is not about relationship, it is about me and only me and there is no second. All relationships on the creature level are selfish. What passes for love there is about convenience and is based solely on the law of mechanical attraction. Attraction is not love. It is the embryonic seed form, the possibility of love. But real love is a process that takes nurturing, time and patience to develop, grow, prosper and mature. At the creature level, this kind of patience does not exist, nor does the understanding required for relationship to develop.

Instead, I am subject to all of the creature impulses that all mammals are subject to without the intervention of conscious volition or conscious labor. There is no development of conscience. These impulses are unconscious and mechanical. They act always and only for the survival of the body and do not consider others. At the creature level, there is basically no such thing as relationship or religion. What is more important, there is no conscious self-control. Thus, in any relationship I am capable of *anything*. I am capable of doing great harm, and I do so, over and over again. If the harm is not physical, then it is verbal, emotional, psychological and spiritual.

Furthermore, at the creature level, the most powerful of all the mechanical impulses is what is called "the survival instinct."

Very few people will be able to tell you precisely of what this instinct is composed. It requires careful study and self observation over a long period of time to expose this mechanism for what it is and to observe the hold which it exerts over my relationships and over my life. My Attention is locked into this mechanism, and whenever there is a moment when I might exert some conscious volition over my behavior, when the survival instinct kicks in, quickly my Attention degenerates into what Collin calls "'fascination' that is into awareness of one thing at a time." This means that at the moment that I surrender to its influence, self remembering becomes impossible. Any awareness of higher influences disappears. My Attention is locked onto one thing only and I cannot remember anything else but the command of the survival instinct.

The Three-Brained Possibility

The human biological instrument is a three-brained creature; it is a mammalian creature. The Being is a non-human entity embodied in a mammal instrument. As far as I can tell, humans are the only three-brained creatures on the planet. This gives us a special possibility which other creatures lack: the third brain, or neo-cortex, provides us with the possibility of thinking for ourselves, knowing ourselves, and remembering ourselves. No other mammals have such a capability.

All mammals are herd animals. Thus, by their very nature they do not think for themselves. The herd thinks for me, the herd speaks for me, and the herd acts for me. If the dominant herd leader leads the herd over a cliff to certain destruction, we follow without question. Witness the creation of nuclear weapons, war of all kinds, gangs, drugs (including cigarettes and alcohol), and the destruction of the environment for profit.

But the survival instinct is not in the mechanical control of the neo-cortex; only when the Being becomes more conscious is there the possibility of conscious management of the survival instinct.

The first neural development in the uterine-being is the development of the spinal system, and connected to it, the first and most primitive of our three brains—the hypothalamus or what biology calls the "reptilian brain." It is important to understand its physical location and the implications of this location. The hypothalamus sits right on top of the spine. Thus, it has direct access to the central nervous system and controls it by instinct. Its intelligence is instinctive intelligence. It does not reason. It reacts to threat to the organism by one of two primitive responses: fight or flight, and those two attendant emotions: anger or fear. This is called the survival instinct. It is the "first responder" in any and all crisis situations: pain or the possibility or threat of pain, whether real or imagined, triggers this mechanical and rapid reaction. What is more, this instinct is always and only selfish.

Dr. Peter Whybrow, author of *American Mania,* explained:

> "The human brain evolved . . . in an environment of scarcity . . . [it is] fabulously limited. We've got the core of the average lizard." Wrapped around this reptilian core . . . is a mammalian layer (associated with maternal concern and social interaction), and around that is wrapped a third layer, which enables feats of memory and the capacity for abstract thought. "The only problem," he says, "is our passions are still driven by the lizard core. We are set up to acquire as much as we can of things we perceive as scarce, particularly sex, safety, and food . . . "The more the lizard core is used the more dominant it becomes. "What we're doing is minimizing the use of the part of the brain that lizards don't have,"

says Whybrow. "We've created physiological dysfunction. We have lost the ability to self-regulate." —Vanity Fair, November 2011, 225.

Even so, in mammals, unlike in lower creatures, a second brain (the thalamus) developed over that first primitive brain. Biology calls this second brain the "mammal brain." Unlike the reptilian brain, which knows only two basic emotions, fear and anger, this mammal brain introduces a new possibility which I will call "nurturing" and Dr. Whybrow calls "maternal concern." This instinct, when developed, is capable of overriding (but not consciously managing) the survival instinct in order to ensure the survival of the infant creature. But we all know that this nurturing instinct is, in many humans, very weak or even non-existent, and more so now in men than in women, although there are many, many women in whom it is weak or non-existent as well. Nevertheless, in all of us, regardless of gender, the first responder is always the hypothalamus or survival instinct. It acts always and only for my own benefit, not others'.

Locating the Survival Instinct

So where exactly in the human biological instrument is this survival instinct located? The survival instinct is located at the instinctive center, which is at the navel, where we were joined to our mothers, the point of contact with the matrix which is our survival mechanism. The instinctive center, as far as I am able to observe, is by far the fastest of all the energy centers in the body. When I am walking down the path through the tall grass to the river to drink, and a snake is coiled to strike beside me, it is the instinctive center which throws the body—literally throws it—out of harm's way. Only then does the emotional center, far slower to respond—it can only respond to the past, to what has already taken place—go into action and flood the body with fear, but too late to save my life. And then, much later, along comes the intellectual center like a stumbling drunk and begins to analyze and label and categorize and "think about" what has just happened and to make generalizations about it: "Oh my God!" it will say, "I'm never going down to the river for a drink again!"

Rage and Terror at the Mammal Level

This "survival instinct is composed of two genuine feelings—not emotions; they come later, after feelings have responded to the present and done their work—and these feelings are rage and terror. Accompanying these two genuine feelings are appropriate corresponding actions: fight and flight. They are triggered by the instinctive production of adrenaline from the adrenal glands, which momentarily gives me superhuman strength and endurance. I am able to run faster, or fight harder, whichever is the most conducive to survival, than I ever have before.

This survival instinct is hardwired into the central nervous system and exists for one reason only: the physical survival of the human biological instrument, nothing else. It does not, cannot, is not constructed to, consider the feelings, needs or survival of others. It is always and only about "I, me, my."

Now here is the interesting thing about this instinct: there was a time when it was totally necessary on a daily, or even a moment-to-moment basis. But that was long ago and, unless I live in the gang- and drug-infested inner city ghetto of some major U.S. city, or in some other situation where my survival is regularly threatened, it is no longer appropriate or necessary on a daily basis. However, the instinctive center does not know this, because it does not think. And the mind which houses the memory of real feeling—rage and terror—now mimics these in the form of shadow emotions: anger and fear. What is more, the instinctive center makes no distinction between real and imagined danger—it responds to pain or the threat—the possibility—of pain, whether real or imagined, always in exactly the same way: fight or flight. To the instinctive center, $A=A=A$, and there is no B. All threats or imagined threats are equal and elicit the same response: fight or flight.

There are seven billion humans on this planet, and for the vast majority of us, this is the way we conduct our relationships: at any hint of pain, or the possibility of pain, the fight-or-flight survival instinct is triggered and we act accordingly. The survival instinct thinks for me, it speaks for me, and it acts for me. Thus, I live most of my life, and act mostly in relationships, ruled by the reptilian brain. All nations act on this level alone. I live a creature life on the lowest creature level. If you hurt me, I hurt you back, either verbally, emotionally, or physically. I am a reactive-mechanism living on the level of a reptile.

No relationship can possibly survive on any sane level when the response to pain or the possibility of pain is such a habitual response. The inevitable result is constant fighting, conflict, hostility, and break-up, which in the U.S. translates to one of the highest divorce rates in the world; over 50 percent of marriages in this country end in divorce. What is more, one in four households in this country are single-parent households. What this means mostly is that the women are left alone to raise the children. The men are reduced to sperm-bearers and, like all reptiles, once they have delivered the sperm, they abandon the offspring.

Conscious Management of the Survival Instinct

The hypothalamus rules my life and my relationships, and only a conscious Being has the possibility of choosing another response, not reacting to the commands of the hypothalamus, but acting consciously according to aim. This requires first of all that at the moment of conflict or pain—the moment the impression enters—I must remember myself and keep the body consciously relaxed. I must eat the impression (see Chapter 9). Otherwise I am simply a habitual creature living a creature's life. In a conscious Being it is possible to manage the survival instinct for the good of another and for the good of the relationship. This conscious management, in which I consider not my feelings only, but the feelings of the other, is an act of conscience. It feeds conscience and allows it to grow. It is an act of non-judgmental love and therefore it feeds our Creator. It helps to maintain the creation, transforming the survival energy in the body into a finer substance which moves back up the food chain to our sun and to the Supreme. In so doing, the human being fulfills the role it was born to fill; a food source for God. One serves God.

Conscious Sacrifice

Non-judgmental love is sacrificial love. In order to act in this sacrificial way, it is necessary for me to sacrifice my judgments of others and act from aim, not from instinct: *Take no position regarding the arising of phenomena; do not react to impressions, or express negativity.* This is the way of the conscious Being, one who manages the mammal body, trains it, tames it in order that it may act in its own higher capacity, as a transformational instrument in the service of our Creator. The Being within must remember itself, consciously place itself—as Attention—below the neck, down lower in the body where it is not identified with the movements of the intellectual-emotional complex, and consciously manage the urge to revenge or to survive, which is the motivation of the survival instinct. This is a sacrificial act; it is the wish to serve. The Being senses the breath, senses the body, and relaxes the body; it issues the invitation, invokes Divine influence.

In order to do this, years of practice are necessary. Self remembering does not come easily as I am formed by this society in which I live. Conscious aim arises only from struggle, suffering, experience and self observation. My aim is kindness. It does not come easily to a man like me, who was raised by a cruel man, and therefore I have a cruel streak in me. I am, like all of us, ruled by self-importance. In my case, self-importance takes the form of self-hatred. It is the opposite side of the coin of arrogance. So the conscious management of the survival instinct requires that I know myself, that I have practiced self observation for many years, and that I have seen how the survival instinct manifests, how hot it comes and how rapidly it takes over the body—it is after all hardwired into the central nervous system for the survival of the organism. So it is strong. My wish must be just as strong, so that this very powerful rush of adrenaline becomes an inner reminding factor which leads me at once to aim, and helps me remember myself and my aim through conscious placement of Attention, sensing the breath, sensing the body, and relaxing the body (first-stage self remembering). Or, *if I am caught and taken*, but understand the process and recognize it when I am caught, then it becomes possible at that moment to find my breath, which then can bring me back to the present, to remembering myself.

I have come, through years of work with self observation, to fear, even respect and value, the mechanical, habitual reactions of my body and the pain which they bring to myself and others. Madame Ouspensky taught me this remarkable insight:

> *All work is based on watchfulness. The man who works realizes he is a machine and fears his machine. Therefore he*

watches. While there is a guardian at the door those who go in and out can be scrutinized . . . A healthy cell does this work by itself . . . Laymen, novices, saints or perfect men, they can all be known by their reactions. His reactions show where a man stands.

—*Talks by Madame Ouspensky,* 1.

It is my reactions which reveal my understanding, my level of consciousness. When I come to fear, respect, value—yes, and even love—my mechanical reactions, the reactions of a machine without conscious volition and self control, only then will I begin the real work to tame and train, to consciously manage, the biological instrument, the mammal, the creature. It can develop self-worth by obedience to the wish of the Being, by service to something higher. "I wish to serve" is the statement of aim of an awakened Being.

The Way of Failure

The conscious management of the survival instinct in the service of aim, in my case kindness, is a high level of work indeed. It is an act of conscience, and it provides conscience with a fine and rich food by which it may develop. One will fail over and over. One begins again. Remorse comes to him who wishes to be kind and fails. This remorse transforms the Being, but this requires that I remain present and consciously assimilate incoming impressions without being taken by the mechanical reaction to them. I cannot remain present because I do not have a sufficient store of impressions of myself to see how I am captured by the distractions of the mind and emotions. Thus, I have no force of accumulated impressions to fuel my wish to remain present. By such accumulation I see my helplessness, and eventually I will never forget, because the shock of seeing and feeling myself as I am is cumulative. As I am, I can change nothing; I cannot "do." But by conscious placement of Attention at the solar plexus, sensing the breath and staying with the breath, sensing the whole body and relaxing it, I allow our Creator to enter. I invite non-judgmental love to do its transformative work in me. In other words, I assume the feminine position in relation to our Creator. I place myself in the position to receive, active-passivity. I consciously receive help from Above. I remain in place in the present, where all transformation takes place. Remorse is the tool which our Creator uses for this transformation. In its higher, conscious function, the human biological instrument is a transformational instrument, an alchemical factory changing powerful but crude energy of revenge into a finer substance: Attention or non-judgmental love. This helps to create an energetic body to house Attention, an "inner structure."

This sacrificial act is a high level of self remembering and involves a great struggle to remember myself and my aims. There will be many failures. One begins again, over and over. This is a great humbling process. My self-importance dies one grain at a time—not all at once, but slowly. With each conscious effort a grain of consciousness is added to Attention so it grows and matures. No conscious effort is ever lost (Madame de Salzmann). It accrues homeopathically over time as I work within.

Apology and Forgiveness

What does such a conscious management of the survival instinct look like on a practical, everyday level? It looks like two things: apology and forgiveness.

Apology and forgiveness are acts of conscience. These are the acts which clear conscience and allow it to grow. They feed conscience. What gets fed, grows—that is the law. Apology and forgiveness are sacrificial acts, done in the service of something higher and finer, something which cannot be named but may be sensed, felt, and experienced. A real man, a human being, is known by his reactions. He is known not by what others say about him, but by what he says about others. He is known by acts of kindness and humility. He is known by his ability to apologize and forgive. This is how non-judgmental love manifests in the human reality. The conscious management of the survival instinct is the practice of a lifetime. It never ends. It comes to me as the result of remorse and fear of hurting others, which have brought about the aim of kindness in me.

And—because if one has read this far, one has paid the price, made the sacrifice, and engaged in the struggle—it is possible to share a revelation which, when it was given to me seemed to be the greatest miracle. Here are the connections which insight and inspiration gave to me regarding this process of apology and forgiveness:

The first thing: the conscious placement of Attention lower down in the body is in fact an act of conscience—it is the Being acting in accordance with the urging of conscience. The practice of Presence awakens and develops conscience in me.

The second thing: once I begin to practice self observation from this new location in the body, conscience is revealed in me. I am allowed to see and feel the urgings of conscience—not as words, but as a small, still feeling: a kind of urgency which points me always and truly toward my own basic goodness (Chögyam Trungpa) and toward non-judgmental love.

The third thing: in its urgings, conscience slowly reveals what I must do in order to keep conscience clear: apologize and forgive. These two simple (but never easy, at least for me) tools are all that is required to clean and clear conscience when I stray from its straight and narrow path. And this clearing process begins with forgiving myself and with inner apology. Who exactly apologizes to whom, inside me? Well, the first apology is from the Being to the body, for all it has been made to bear of the demands and desires of me-myself. The second apology, at the quiet, gentle, and wise urging of conscience, is from the Being to our Creator for the harm I have done, to self and others.

The fourth thing—and for me this is where the miraculous intervened—is this revelation: conscience is a compass needle which always and in everything points toward true north = goodness and non-judgmental love. God is goodness and non-judgmental love. Therefore, conscience is the will of God in me! The will of God is not somewhere in the sky. That is too childish, ignorant and foolish. If it were somewhere outside of me it would be of no value to me. The will of God is within every single human ever born on this planet, and it is conscience. That is why conscience never lies and can be counted on absolutely, in every situation.

And finally, the fifth thing: real faith arises from this understanding. I have found in me that which can always, and in everything, be trusted. I have found where, and in what, to place my faith. And it is not blind faith, it is not faith placed in me by others, it is not faith from doctrines or belief systems or books. It is faith which arises from lived experience, from living truth revealed through the urging of conscience in the present. Once one discovers where and what exactly the will of God is, one has found the path out of hell. Is this not truly wonderful? Is this not miracle enough?

The great Tibetan Buddhist Master Chögyam Trungpa Rinpoche taught his senior disciples this highest of work teachings: "If kindness doesn't work, try more kindness." This is the practice of one who has gained an inner strength born of sacrifice and understanding. Madame Ouspensky taught, "While there is a guardian at the door those who go in and out may be scrutinized . . . a healthy cell does this work by itself." This "guardian at the door" could be taken as Attention at the top of the head, guarding incoming energetic impressions, those pulsations or impulses, before the mind can steal them and turn them into thought. Lord have mercy; I wish to work.

> *The single greatest technique for work on Self is to endure*
> *the unpleasant manifestations of others without resentment,*
> *expressions of displeasure, or the demand for intelligence,*
> *reason, justice or conscience on the part of others. Endure*
> *silently and cheerfully and suffer in the stew pot of tension.*
> —E. J. Gold, *The Joy of Sacrifice*

> *First—one can learn to accept displeasing manifestations*
> *originating in others and in the environment without becom-*
> *ing either inwardly or outwardly agitated or resentful. This*
> *provides real material useful for "fanning the sparks of the*
> *purifying fire" which fuses the centers into a unified entity.*
> — E.J. Gold. *The Joy of Sacrifice*, 69-70.

> *It was so cold in Manhattan today, the flashers in Times*
> *Square were just describing themselves to people.*
> —David Letterman

The Cost of Killing the Animals

The Earth is a sentient Being, with
a vast intelligence and a vital body:
organic life is its organ system,
trees its lungs, water its blood, and we

are its nervous system. Each organ
gives off a unique force crucial
to the life of the body. If one organ dies,
another must take over its function

or the Earth dies.
We are killing off the animals, so
humans must assume their function
which means massive numbers of us

must live like dogs, only
without a dog's devotion,
lacking a dog's courage or loyalty.
We must live lives of simple brutality

and constant sexual tension.
We must reproduce in vast numbers
to replace the slaughtered animals.
We must pay by becoming them,

(continued with stanza break)

living like lizards,
breaking our children,
dying like dogs.
That is the Law and

we are bound to it
the way a dog
is bound by a chain
to a tree.

— Red Hawk. *The Art of Dying*, 8

CHAPTER 13

Self Observation

Buddha says, "A master gives up all mischief." . . . Because a master gives up mind. Mind is mischief; there is no other mischief. Mind is the source of all mischief. A master is a master only because he has ceased to be dominated by the mind. A master is a master of himself; he is no longer unconscious . . . (199) [T]he only way to disconnect yourself from the past is to disconnect yourself from your mind because your mind is the past. Mind means the known, the past. Mind is history, mind is time . . . and unless you get out of the hold of the mind, whatsoever you do is going to be mischievous . . . Out of mind, nothing good can ever happen. (201)

—Osho. *The Dhammapada*

Knowing others is wisdom; /Knowing the self is enlightenment./ Mastering others requires force;/ Mastering the self needs strength.// He who knows he has enough is rich./ Perseverance is a sign of will power./ He who stays where he is endures./ To die but not to perish is to be eternally present.

—Lao Tsu. *Tao Te Ching*. Thirty-three.

Two things are required to operate in the human biological instrument, as well as in all other possible worlds or realities, with maximum effectiveness and efficiency: Presence and Attention (E.J. Gold. *Life in the Labyrinth*, 161). These are the two essential qualities or aspects of Being. Without both things I operate unconsciously as a mammal with a mammal's habits; that is, repetitively and inefficiently. Self remembering invokes Presence; self observation invokes Attention. These two states are lawful states for efficient movement and appropriate behavior in all worlds, including the physical and the *bardo*-worlds (those after-death realms). In other words, whatever reality I find myself in—in or outside of a physical body—these two states are self-sufficient and appropriate orientation.

Now, at last, we may speak of self observation. Before self observation comes self remembering. It must be this way. Unless I remember myself, unless I invoke Presence, how can I observe myself? And I wish to observe myself always in relationship—with the body, with others, with my surroundings, and with the guru and our Creator. Human life is relationship. I come here as a being whose qualities are Presence and Attention in order to learn how to be in right relationship with our Creator, which is the now, and only exists as here-now. So self observation must take place in the present in order to be in relationship with the Source, and thus to grow and mature the Being, which is Presence and Attention. Self observation is a function of Attention.

> *When I try, it is now. I try that none of my attention goes into up or down, past or future—only now.*
> —Henriette Lannesm, *Inside a Question*, 159.

Attention is a point in a field. Consciousness—which is the domain of the guru and is God—is the field in which all phenomena arise. Attention is a point in that field. Each of us is such a point in the field of consciousness. We are a charged particle in that field. But I remain charged only so long as I remain present in that field, which is now. Thus, when I speak of "field Attention," I am speaking of a moment when the point unites with the field, which is its matrix. The separation is ended and there is a unified field. Physicists, including Albert Einstein, have struggled to discover the "Unified Field Theory" when it was always right under their noses, but must include the inner world, which physics cannot acknowledge because it cannot be verified by external experimentation. Self remembering and self observation, taken together, eventually lead to a unified field in which self merges once again into God or non-judgmental love. The point is unified with the field. "I am" is surrendered into love. This can only happen with the grace and mercy of God and the guru. I cannot will it, force it, or make it happen. But I can place myself in the position of active-passivity in which I cease to interfere with the work of our Creator, thus allowing its grace and mercy to manifest in the human being. That position is the present, here now. The present is the source of all possibility. *The destination is the present—it must be constantly renewed with every breath or the connection is lost.*

The Recoil into Fear

One of self observation's central functions is the collection and storing of impressions of my unconscious, habitual mechanicality; in this, the memory is a very useful storage tool. Slowly, slowly self observation reveals my strategic retreat from the present, from the now of the body, because I live in terror. It is the way I avoid relationship and it is the movement of fear, the refusal to accept *what is, as it is, here and now*, the refusal to see and feel the terror of my situation because I am afraid of it. It is this recoil into fear which is, in fact, what I call "myself."

Ordinary human life, mammal life, is therefore composed almost exclusively of distractions from this reality due to fear of what it contains, a continuous movement away from the present in which this self-created terror might be seen and felt. What is more, it does not matter to the mind whether these distractions are attractive or repulsive, so long as they keep me from seeing and feeling the "terror of the situation." This recoil into fear, known as the self, is what is added onto reality; thus, the teaching is to relax into reality and allow Attention to expand and merge into the field of consciousness, which is the present.

I am terrified of the unknown present, in which life and love arise, and I cling to this terror despite all the evidence of a lifetime that such clinging is self-destructive and insane. I prefer the insanity I know to the love which is unknown. Thus dawns a wish. The feeling-pain which arises from this strategic retreat into fear gives birth to the real wish to be present, where all help and love exist. But this wish does not have strength for a long time; it is easily overcome by the force and habit of fear. Madame de Salzmann has taught that the slow and patient accumulation of impressions supports this wish. I become ever more conscious of my mechanicality—my unconscious, habitual reliance on the mechanism of fear to protect me from reality, from love, from God and the guru: from the unknown, which is outside the mind.

Self observation slowly reveals the mind's fear-based, constant movement to distract Attention from its natural and easeful resting in the present, its matrix of consciousness where the point may naturally bond and merge into the field. The mind's constant restless movement is a strategic retreat from the body and the breath, which are always and only present. The practice of self remembering/self observation is the gentle, non-judgmental means of correcting this separation, this dis-ease, of allowing Attention to rest in its matrix or safe place, of restoring it to its Divine Mother consciousness, the Sacred Heart of Mercy, which is non-judgmental love, always and only present. Self observation collects impressions of my unconsciousness over a long period of time, and this slow accretion of impressions gives will to wish so that I do not forget—forget my practice, forget why I work, or forget the suffering attendant upon refusal to work. It supports the wish to be present.

"myself" as a Collection of Memories

What self observation revealed to me was that what I knew and called "myself" was a collection of memories; it was the collected personal history of this particular mammal, endlessly repeating. At the center of this collection of memories was what the Work calls "chief feature." Chief feature is the organizing principle for this collection. In my case, the organizing principle is self-hatred. Chief feature manifests mainly as self-importance or self-pity; self-hatred is one aspect of self-importance. One of the great traps of finally uncovering this chief feature or blind spot is that I first become fascinated by it, and finally obsessed with it. Thus the practice is to expand Attention, including both the inner reactions and the outer phenomena.

> *Some Gates [to Paradise] comprise challenges which provide necessary conditions for souls whose natures are not perfected, and which act by using the imperfection as a means of transformation. The greater the seeming imperfection, the greater the possible transformation.*
>
> —author unknown. Quoted in an email from a friend

Self remembering/self observation is a self-correcting mechanism. I have said this many times but the implications of this are vast. It means that self observation will reveal those places in me in which I am holding on or identified, thus preventing the flow of love energy to manifest in the body. Such revelations are very painful emotionally and psychologically. What is revealed may require that I get the help of trained professionals in order to come to terms with, and accept without judgment, what self observation reveals. Help is available if I have the courage to see and feel when I need it, and then ask for it. But I must first see and feel, for a long time, my helplessness in the face of my addictions—physical, psychological and emotional. I must see and feel that my life as I am is out of control and that I cannot remain present.

Urgency and Necessity

When various "i's" begin to arise as the buffer system is dismantled, and the suffering becomes intense enough, only then do two things arise which are of enormous help in the inner work: urgency and necessity. When I am drowning, I will take whatever help is made available to me, and I will use all of my resources in order to survive. This has been the case with me. It became a matter of life and death. My years of work were threatened by the arising of certain "i's" in me which did not care if they sabotaged my work, my livelihood or my life. Therefore, I had to work and practice as if my life depended upon it. It does. Zen calls this level of practice "Practicing as if your hair were on fire." Am I willing to die in order to do this work?

Once this level of urgency arises, a person may arrive at the point where he sees that life on the mammal level, driven by unconscious urges and reactions, by a life of survival habits, is no longer viable—at which point he may arrive at a point in the

Work which signals a shift in context and a change in attitude: "I have had enough." Now one may say this in fact many times in his or her life and mean it in the moment, but always slip back into unconscious habits, which indicates that one has *not* had enough. It is not yet a question of life or death. What Mister E. J. Gold pointed out is that, once a person reaches this point in the Work, clinging to even the smallest thing in my body of habits—it may seem utterly inconsequential—will draw me right back into the mammal life, back into the entrapment of identification. This is crucial to understand: "In for a penny, in for a pound." Mister Lee has said that if there is even 1-percent identification, there is 100-percent identification. Now, everything matters, and the only thing which will save me in this situation, in which truly "I have had enough," is radical reliance on the guru (or God).

Having reached this stage of necessity and urgency, I may fear that I do not have the strength of will to maintain my inner position and be present to the Presence within. What I have seen is that, when the intention is fueled by real feeling, will arises in me to meet the need. Call it "grace." For example, when I had practiced expanded or split Attention for a significant time, taking in my inner state, my surroundings and the guru or God or consciousness, completing the inner triad, my breathing changed. It became deeper and slower sometimes. Observation showed me that breath begins to take part in this purification process by clearing out the frontal bodily channel by which breath may fill and penetrate the entire body. It ceases to be merely shallow, tense chest breathing and begins to move downward to fill the channel to the base of the spine and the abdomen. When it is doing this, there is the bodily urge to take fuller, deeper breaths down into the abdomen, to purify this channel. When this is happening, Attention naturally moves to the abdomen and the base of the spine. At other times, the breath moves to energize the heart center, at which time Attention moves to that area. It also moves up the spine to the top of the head so it appears to be enlivening the entire channel from the top of the head to the base of the spine, so that breath becomes conscious Being-food and at the same time aids in the purification of the center channel of the body. It knows what to do so long as I do not interfere. Then, just as naturally—as it does in my case—Attention comes back to its center of gravity at the solar plexus. In you, it may rest elsewhere. But the point is that the will to stay present arises—not all the time of course, but far more often than before, and then the process of purification takes hold and the body knows what to do. The body becomes a transformational instrument as the result of the pressure exerted upon it by consistent and unrelenting Presence and Attention being placed upon it.

At this point, I must live in the present as much as is possible, in the now of the body, which is the guru's domain. I must live in God-alone, which is here now. And I cannot do so without the grace and mercy of the guru/God. My intention must be focused and sincere and with powerful wish from the emotional center behind it—mind alone will not do. This is where self remembering and self observation are crucial. I become extremely watchful, observant, and utilize what the body of habits gives me to remember myself. Certain inner movements become like electric shocks and serve as inner reminding factors to bring me to Awareness and awakening to be present to the Presence within. Having reached a certain stage in the Practice of Presence, the practice of expanded Attention—in which I am aware of myself externally and am consciously relaxing the body, as well as being aware within, observing and catching each inner reaction as it arises and before it can reach my will, as my friend Lalitha so beautifully puts it—becomes crucial. It allows me to utilize every inner movement to return to Presence and remain relaxed into the here-now, where the guru lives and works to transform the Being. By doing my work, I allow the guru/God/Love to do Its work.

Inner Reminding Factors

By catching each inner movement, which is the action of "myself," several reminding factors become a source of real help. These three inner reminding factors are: i. unnecessary thinking, ii. inappropriate emotions, and iii. unnecessary tension.

i. unnecessary thinking

The first such inner reminding factor is unnecessary thinking. Unnecessary thinking is any thought which occurs mechanically and without the conscious volition and intention of the Being—that is, random, habitual thinking, imagination, day dreaming, fantasy, like that. All unnecessary, random thinking is the movement of recoil into fear and is a distraction from the present. Fear is a movement away from the present. Thought is a movement away from the present because all thought is from the known, which is memory, and memory is a past-future mechanism only.

Necessary thinking, that is, thought which is an efficient function of the mind, involves mainly three functions. The first function is solving technical problems in the present. (The mind is a problem-solving tool and is very efficient at this function. It is a necessary function.) The second function is communication. (The mind is the storehouse of language and is efficient at using it to communicate with others, as I am doing here. This too is a necessary function.) And finally, the mind—which is memory—is good at remembering. It is necessary in self remembering. I remember myself and my practice and then conscious intention takes over from that point, shifting Attention to the now of the body once I see that I have been caught in unnecessary thinking; thus, unnecessary thinking becomes an inner reminding factor, an ally and advisor.

> *I do not let myself be carried away by a dangerous need to know more. This need will be my undoing. I put all my trust in a note that vibrates more clearly and more fully: I AM AT-TENTION. Then, everything I thought I understood, with my intellect, for example—everything that would have taken me off course—I will know directly . . . Attention is like a thread that passes through all levels. And this thread is: I AM ATTENTION.*
>
> *Do you need anything more?*
>
> —Michel Conge. *Inner Octaves*, 153.

What follows below is Mister Lee's commentary on this quote from Michel Conge:

> *We have come to this extraordinary point, this direct experience of "what is, as it is, here and now", of "Just this". The moment is sparkling with pure magic . . . [and] the mind says: "What is this? Why is this? How can this be used? How can I get/have more?" and we are carried <u>away</u>. We are ripped from the here and now and taken back to a reflective, investigative, self-referenced space, so distant and so foreign from that pure, pristine place of "Just This", of IS, that we are undone, fully and effectively. And sometimes this "need to know more" is so consuming, so <u>habitual,</u> that we don't even cognize the fact that we have been carried <u>away,</u> that the Life we had felt in that moment has been slaughtered.*

So we must see this tendency in us . . . and in knowing this about ourselves, about our minds, guard against it when it is moving, strategizing to carry us <u>away</u> . . . The quote above is: "<u>I do not let myself</u> . . .," meaning I, the I of consciousness, the I that "accepts what is, as it is, here and now," the Objective I, does have choice, can be in and stay in control, can effectively manage the "I" of "needing to know more" and this I, the unified I, the higher I, does not let the lesser "I" intrude and destroy. To be present is the aim, to be "Just this", to Assert the Reality . . . of existence . . . To be "carried away" is to be distanced, separated from this presence . . . "<u>Do not let yourself</u> be carried away." Do not!
         —Lee Lozowick, *Chasing Your Tail*, 205-206.

The guardian, that portion of Attention which remains sensing at the top of the head, now becomes alert to any unnecessary movement of thought. Unnecessary thinking is a strategy to avoid relationship. Thus, the mere impulse to thought, which arises as an energetic impression before the thought takes active form, serves as the shock to return to the body. This becomes an instant reminding factor and there is an anchoring effect which roots Attention in the body—no movement toward or away from the thought, no identification with the impulse. The guardian remains aware, alert, watchful, observant. This is self observation of an entirely different dimension and with a new, unknown result. The guardian serves the present, serves the guru, serves our Creator. It is "actively passive."

The result is unknown because when Attention is in place in the body it is aligned with the unknown, no personal history, no past, no self as it has been defined and described by my personal history, the known. It is a position of total vulnerability to the guru, the bodily position of surrender. It is not surrender itself. That comes only by the guru's grace and mercy. But it places the Being in the position so that surrender may find me; I am where surrender can take place. I offer the body as prasad to our Creator and guru for its use and in service to it. I am face down in the dust at the feet of the guru. I have leapt into the abyss of nothingness, am nothing, and am at the mercy of the unknown. I am in the position of bodily organic innocence (as Mister Lee taught us) and organic ignorance (as Master Da taught us). This is bodily worship of the descending Divine love current which is always present.

What I have seen is that, with Attention placed in this way, the top of the head and the whole front of the body are open and vulnerable. They open to consciousness and I can sense the descent of a finer energy into the body and around it. This sensation is being present to the Presence within and around and above me. It invites this unknown Presence to take this prasad for its use. It invites a kind of death in surrender, an active-passivity. I place myself at the mercy of the Sacred Heart of Mercy, which is the guru/God, the here-now.

In this way, slowly mind is consciously managed and brought into relationship with the whole body, aligned with the other centers, and feeding the growth of Being. Being grows in direct relationship to the amount of time Attention is in the present (Osho). The struggle to remain present develops the Attention (Madame de Salzmann). There is a gradual breaking of identification with the mechanism as Attention unites with its matrix, which is consciousness. Everything in me aligns with this bonding process. Attention is returning to Source, bonding with its matrix, and becoming one with it, dying to the self and being reborn into the Whole. Unnecessary thought becomes a triggering mechanism to anchor Presence and Attention in the here-now of the body.

This active-passivity represented by the guardian at the top of the head is one thing that is meant by mindfulness. That portion of Attention-sensation at the base of the spine monitors the spine, posture and movement. This is another meaning of mindfulness. Attention-sensation at the top of the head becomes aware of every movement of the mind, and the mind itself becomes full of Awareness, guided not by its own mechanical behavior, but by a force which is in it, but not of it—a force greater than itself. It remains alert and clear, waiting to be used when appropriate and necessary. Otherwise, it is silent and watchful. It is aligned within the Whole and not separate. Sensation unites it: Attention sensing at the top of the head, base of the spine and solar plexus/heart center. Mindfulness creates clarity of vision and thinking. It allows me to appreciate the smallest details of the present moment, and appreciation is the key word here. Gratitude arises spontaneously, deepest wonder and gratitude to being alive in the body of God and the Presence of the guru, which Presence may be sensed at the top of the head, or arising in the heart center and felt at times throughout the entire body.

ii. inappropriate emotions

The second such inner reminding factor is inappropriate emotions. Arnaud Desjardins tells us that Swami Prajnanpad has said that all emotions are false, therefore inappropriate. This is a radical statement which at first appears counter-intuitive. However, careful self observation of emotions brings a certain clarity about them.

What are the emotions and why do they exist? Jan Cox (a teacher of Fourth Way) first instructed me that emotions are a measuring device built into the mechanism in order to reveal certain properties about my present environment. They measure the amount of danger in the environment and are basically four in number: fear, anger, sadness and happiness (or as Eric Berne once put it: mad, sad, glad, scared). The greater the danger in the present, the greater the fear, and then anger (fight or flight). The less danger, the greater the happiness. It eventually becomes even clearer that what the emotions are really measuring on a deeper level is the amount of love present in any given environment. The greater the love, less fear; the less love, more fear. Fear is the bottom line, baseline measurement, default position for the emotions. Everything stems from it. Less fear, more love, like that.

However, Swami Prajnanpad's teaching becomes more apparent as I observe emotions more closely over time. It becomes clear that emotions are a reaction to something which has already taken place—they are a response to the past, thus they are a distraction from the present and are based in fear. The instinctive center, which is much faster than the emotional center, will have already moved the body into action to take care of any real present danger by fight or flight. The emotions are a reaction to this action, an acknowledgement of the danger which was present and is no more. Furthermore, continued self observation reveals that the emotions make absolutely no distinction between real and present danger and imaginary danger or remembered danger from the past, even long past. They react in exactly the same way every time, automatically and mechanically. They do not reason, they merely react, always and everywhere in the same way, habitually.

Finally, the emotions are a shadow world. They are a bodily memory of real feelings such as rage and terror, which abide in the instinctive center; their shadow-memory is anger and fear. It is the same with sadness and happiness. Emotions may linger, even for a lifetime, habitually calling for the same bodily reaction endlessly and with no external stimuli. They are never satisfied and remain constantly calling for inappropriate action to meet their need. Arnaud Desjardins has taught that the unfulfilled needs of the child become the desires of the adult. It is these old desires which emotions so often are responding to, with no possibility of fulfillment.

What is more, Mister Gurdjieff taught that negative emotions, which are so habitual and unceasing in me, are not only *not real*, but they have no center in the body—therefore they use the other centers to manifest their desires. Self observation has revealed the truth of this for me. Negative emotions may arise in the mind, the heart, the navel, or the abdomen. They steal the life energy of the body, thwart the growth of the Being, and consume Attention via identification. Thus, the invaluable teaching of Arnaud from his master Swami Prajnanpad: "Never believe thoughts associated with emotions."

Patient self observation over a long period of time reveals the symbiotic relationship between mind and emotions, which is why I speak of the intellectual-emotional complex. Mind and emotions work together, especially negative emotions, in order to control Attention, capture it, and consume it for their own growth and livelihood. They do not act in the best interest of the body, the life, or the Being within. Their only aim is the restoration, repetition, and replication of themselves. You must not *believe* what I am saying here. These are mere words, they are not experience. By patient self observation, you will learn your own truth about these matters. In all things, I wish to verify for myself, by my own personal experience, what is true about me.

The management of negative emotions, which I speak about in great detail in Chapter 12 regarding the survival instinct, is essential to the growth of the Being. Likewise, the management of mind is equally essential. Unless I am able to become more objective about the mechanical workings of these two mechanisms, I will remain enslaved and trapped within their web all of my life, unable to die consciously.

The breaking of identification with the intellectual-emotional complex is extremely difficult and painful; that is why it is called the Work. It is hard work. It will take years of patient observation to reach the point of "I have had enough." It may take lifetimes. Nevertheless, there is a point in the Work where I have had enough of the mammal life, the mammal reactions, the mammal thinking, and the mammal suffering. Only when I have had enough of the suffering brought about by my identification with the mammal will I begin to deal in an appropriate way with my own negativity, programmed into me in my childhood—and even earlier, in the uterus—and begin to take full responsibility for my life and my behavior. Until then, I remember myself and I observe myself, always learning and growing in the process, developing something inside which is unshakeable and may survive the death of the body without losing its stability. In this way, I build a stable inner structure to house Presence and Attention.

iii. unnecessary tension in the body

Finally, the third such inner reminding factor is unnecessary tension in the body. Every thought, every emotion, every unnecessary thought, every inappropriate emotion, is accompanied by tension in the body, and all of these taken together are the manifestations of this so-called "myself" which I am called on to observe. Tension is how I hold onto the past in the musculature and even the skeletal alignment, the posture. Thus, all unnecessary tension is a distraction from the present and is the result of fear.

This is not to be confused with commonsense necessary tension. I need a certain necessary tension to sit, to stand erect, to walk, to speak, to think when it is necessary, and it goes on.

Necessary tension is simply that tension required to do the job at hand and no more. This is only possible when Attention is in its place in the body, I am mindful, and sensing the whole of the body. Then, as I lift, I do not unnecessarily grit my teeth or lock my jaw. As I shake hands my facial muscles are relaxed—no false unnecessary smile, but open and warm in my vulnerability, eyes wide open. Find out what "eyes wide open" means, literally; see what state this produces.

Most of my life has been spent in unnecessary tension from remembered emotions in childhood and in the womb. These tensions became more or less a permanent part of my inner landscape such that they became invisible to me. Mister Gold has taught that so long as one's sense of self is located in the head, essence manifests in the musculature. Only patient self observation over a long period of time began to reveal just to what extent I lived in a state of permanent anxiety and bodily tension. My back, as I aged, became a mass of tension, my neck and shoulders and back in constant pain. Such bodily tension drains the life force and steals the energy needed for the practice of self observation. It thwarts the growth of the Being because it keeps me locked in the past and therefore unable to maintain a present-Attention which allows the Being to grow.

My Attention is weak and unstable, subject to every kind of inner and outer distraction. I am unable to remain present in the now of the body for even seconds before thought, emotion or bodily tension steal, capture and consume Attention. But the struggle itself, the beautiful and holy struggle to remain ever more present, strengthens Attention, slowly but lawfully. Every moment spent in this struggle is not lost, but added to the force which builds Attention. I relax into the expansion of Attention and into the inevitable contraction as well.

So, moment to moment, I begin again. I sense the tension in parts of my body and I sense the breath. I breathe into those areas and I consciously relax them, when possible. If not possible, I observe where tension is stored and, unable to relax, I accept this and I keep a watchful inner eye on those places. As I sit here typing this manuscript I become aware of the tension in neck, shoulders and back. I breathe more fully, I move the shoulders and neck, I stretch the back, I relax. This kind of mindfulness when doing a physical task is essential to the growth of Attention. It allows me to exert just enough muscular force to do the job at hand, and not tense my calf muscles and thighs [yes, I just noticed that] as I am performing the task. Thus, I become more efficient at the labor I do, and I consciously manage the energetic force in the body, allowing it to become available for inner work. My work is to manage my personal energy—my vibrational field—and to allow life to have free and full reign without manipulation, repression or interference. I eat impressions.

In effect, I become a good farmer, husbanding my resources, diligently preparing the soil to receive the seed, managing the growth of the seed until it blooms into a beautiful flower. A consciously relaxed body is the signal for God/guru to enter; it is the invitation for non-judgmental love to move down and into the body. It will not enter except by invitation alone, and this invitation may only be issued by a conscious Being doing its work of alignment. I wish to serve. A relaxed body is a vulnerable body. I become consciously vulnerable to the guru/God and allow him/it to do the work of transformation in me.

Non-Interference

My place is small in this work, but significant: I must not interfere. Unnecessary thinking, inappropriate emotions and unnecessary tension in the body interfere with the holy work of transformation. They block the free movement of energy required for purification and transformation, and they stop self remembering and self observation so this beautiful, this perfect, self-correcting mechanism cannot perform the function it was created for.

The human being (both aspects: the human and the Being, joined as one) is created first as a food factory, to feed what is higher on the scale of life. Second, the human being was created to operate as a charged particle in a charged field, thus becoming a receiving and transmitting device so that our Creator may communicate with its creation. It does this by finding an open channel through which it may transmit non-judgmental love, my real nature. The Work is to establish a stable charge in the particle, making it able to work and, thus, useful to our Creator.

First comes wish, from the feeling, then comes aim from the mind, then comes practice from the whole of me. It is practice to relax the body and keep unnecessary tension from distorting and aging it too rapidly. Mister Gurdjieff had as one of the aphorisms on the Prieure's Study House wall: "Man is given a definite number of experiences—economizing them he prolongs his life" (*Views from the Real World*, 276). Thus, I husband my resources, economizing my inner force, wasting nothing, so that I may be granted, by God's grace and mercy, a longer time to achieve my aim of building a stable inner structure which can survive the death of the body—a stable Attention with which I may serve our Creator.

This is the creation of a third world: Between the world of the Divine and the world of the human, through conscious labor and voluntary suffering, the world of Being may be created to act as a bridge between these two worlds, which cannot meet except with the reconciling force of this third world.

We are all, such as we are, under the influence of our imagination of ourselves. This influence is all-powerful and conditions every aspect of our lives . . . (155)

I need to learn to recognize and separate the real "I" from the imagination of myself. This is an arduous task because my imagined "I" defends itself. It is opposed to the real "I" . . .

This imagination of "I . . . me" lies at the heart of my usual sense of self, the ego, *and* all the movements of my inner life go to protect it [my emphasis. RH] *. . . There is no thought or feeling that is not motivated by this. It is, however, so subtle that we do not see it . . . But today the controlling influence is the idea of myself, and this imagined "I" desires, fights, compares and judges all the time. It wants to be . . . recognized, admired and respected . . .*

Do I know this? Not just in passing, or in having noticed it one day or another . . . but do I really see it at the moment in each action, when I work, when I eat, when I speak with another person? Can I be aware of my wish to be "someone" and my way of always comparing myself to another? . . . So long as I have not understood that this is the essence of my search, that here is the first step (156) *toward knowledge of myself, I will continue to be fooled and all my efforts, all the ways I try to change, will lead only to disappointment. The imagined "I," my imagination of "I," will continue to be reinforced even in the most unconscious layers of myself.*

I must honestly accept that I really do not know this. Only in accepting this as a fact will I become interested and truly wish to know it. Then my thoughts, feelings and actions will no longer be objects for me to look at with indifference. They are me, *expressions of my* self, *which I alone am*

here to understand. If I wish to understand them, I must live with them, not as a spectator but with affection, and without judging or excusing them. It is necessary to live with my thoughts, feelings and actions, to suffer them, from moment to moment. (157)
　　　　　—Jeanne de Salzmann, *The Reality of Being.*

This so-called myself is a mental concept, an imaginative construct, a strategy to avoid relationship, a recoil from reality into fear. Every thought, emotion and action is a manifestation of this myself. And myself is ruthless, without mercy, with no consideration for self or others, without conscience, totally selfish and acting always and only in its own interest. If I understand this—that is, see and feel it and suffer it—and I do so "with affection, and without judging or excusing them [my thoughts, feelings, and actions]," then what occurs is a shift in the context in which I view "myself."

The shock of understanding and seeing this now, here, even as you are reading this book, can blow the mind and throw it into silence. It is right that this bomb lays in wait until this point in the book. One must pay to receive such a shock as this. One must be prepared. And in the quote from Madame lies the hidden key: observation "with affection." Not just without judgment, but with a feeling which recognizes and respects the value of my negativity! Herein lies freedom.

Thus, when the old wave of negativity sweeps over me, I make real effort to remain present, in the now of the body. I trust this. I trust that Presence and Attention will be enough to get me through, and so I am able to simply *be*, with nothing special added to it, just present and open to relationship as I am: no personality, no myself, no personal history, no ego-structure added to what is, as it is, here and now; just this. As I am is enough. Something old must die in order for something new to be born: the old becomes fodder for new growth. Don't be afraid.

> *The destination is the present—it must be constantly renewed with every breath or the connection is lost.*

(Note: For further discussion of self observation, please see *Self Observation: The Awakening of Conscience. An owner's manual.* Prescott, Arizona: Hohm Press, 2010.)

> *I've always been crazy, but it's kept me from going insane.*
> —Waylon Jennings

The Way of Attention

Buddha says that 3 actions determine life.

i. breath

The wise woman observes her breath, conserves it,
follows it as the shadow follows the body,
is reserved, speaks only when necessary;
her speaking follows the 4 Imperatives:
kind, truthful, helpful, necessary, otherwise
she keeps her own counsel;
this is mastery of tongue.

ii. impressions

The wise woman observes impressions
without judgment or clinging,
impersonally the way the Sun
shines on all living things without favor;
she guards the impression she leaves with others,
showing only those feathers
suitable to the occasion;
she shows all her feathers only with good reason,
to birds of her own kind, everything in its season;
this is mastery of mood.

iii. sensations

The wise woman observes her body, studies its functions
and tames them the way the hunter
tames a good dog to follow her lead;
taming the senses, she is freed of excess,
practices moderation in all things, no need
to indulge in drifting thoughts, moods,

or the shifting desires of the body;
this is mastery of the form.

Buddha says that the total cessation of the 3 actions
defines death. It is a wise woman who has mastered
tongue, mood and form; she has mastered Attention,
over which death has no dominion. She alone is free.

Red Hawk, *Mother Guru*, 171

Epilogue: Practice of the Dharma

Practice of the Dharma

Some men climb the highest mountains
and they endure terrible hardships;
some men go to war where they see
and endure unimaginable suffering;
some men pursue money, sex, power,
fame or drugs and for them there is
no end to the pain and longing of the spirit.
But woe unto him who finds the Dharma
and seeks to Practice what he learns there,
for the suffering he must endure
cannot be spoken; the hardships
he must endure are more terrible than
all others and his spirit will be broken;
he will be left trembling and afraid, naked
as the worst addict, bereft as the poorest beggar,

troubled and shamed as the whoremonger
and the thief.
Do not undertake to Practice the Dharma friend,
I warn you, I implore you, I beg you, for
you will be found out,
your secrets will be exposed as if they were
the common gossip in the bars and alleys
of hell. Everything which you hold dear
will be taken from you and you will be
left weeping and gnashing your teeth,

alone as the day you entered this world and
more naked because even your innocence

will be taken from you and you will be
thrown at the feet of God with nothing,
nothing to clothe you, nothing to sustain you,
nothing but your Practice of the Dharma and
friend, it will exact from you the last and

most precious coin held tight in your
sweating hand. On this trip a man may
take nothing with him, nothing
will accompany him save his Practice.
The Dharma is a terrible Master; all
who undertake it must die; no one
has ever survived.

— Red Hawk, *Mother Guru*, 106

Postlude: Angel of Mercy

Angel of Mercy

Help me Master, the levee has broken
and I've nowhere else to go but You.
Help me. These are the truest words I've spoken;
if there's no room in Your boat, I'm through,

it's over, the flood waters will cover me.
My house is floating downstream
and I don't know what's come over me,
every prayer I offer is a scream:

Help me Master! Mind can't understand,
the levee's broken and there's no dry land,
the gators and the snakes are close at hand
and nothing's going the way I'd planned.

Help me master, that's my only prayer;
it is on every breath,
my heart is broken, I am ruined, stripped bare
and the only friend I have save You is death,

so help me please, I know who You are.
You're the Angel of Mercy and You've come like fire
to light the way through darkness, a burning star;
I sing your praises like a broken, ruined choir.

All my levees were built on sand,
they gave way in the high wind and
rising tide. Desperate times demand
desperate measures; help me or I am damned.

Red Hawk, *Mother Guru,* 58

Coda

The master cannot react. He responds, but he never reacts. Reactions come from the past, response is spontaneous; it is in the present…the conscious man responds.…His action is born out of the present.

And remember one fundamental secret of life: if the action is born out of the present it is never binding; if it comes out of the past it is binding, it is karma. If the action comes out of your present awareness it is not karma, it is not binding. You do it and it is finished, you do it and you get out of it; it never accumulates in you. The master never accumulates the past; he dies every moment to the past. He is born anew every moment.

—Osho Rajneesh. *The Dhammapada,* 24

Amo Ergo Sum

Glossary

Aim: the conscious creation of an inner Work-purpose; an inner Work-related goal, based on one's continued self observation. Aim comes from intellectual center (see: **Centers**) and can arise from **Wish.**

Attention: the act of focusing the mind, feelings, and Being on an object or process. The Being is Attention in a human body; consciousness (see also: **Being**).

Basic Goodness: the true Being-nature unencumbered by ego-interference; the Being instructed and guided by **Conscience** (suggested by Chögyam Trungpa Rinpoche).

Being: called variously soul, atman, spirit; it is Attention or **Consciousness**, undeveloped in ordinary life, developed only through special effort, conscious effort (see also: **Attention**).

Blind Spot: see **Chief Feature**

Buffer: a mental/psychological/emotional assemblage by which Attention is directed away from one's inner contradictions, lies, habits, and mechanical reactions, so that they remain hidden from awareness.

Centers: Some systems might call these *chakras, points of energy transformation* in the body. Here we consider mainly four centers: intellectual (head-brain), emotional (solar plexus-heart center), instinctive (navel), and moving (base of the spine). The Work also teaches of two higher intellectual and emotional centers, which exist outside of, but connected to and accessible by, the body.

Chief Feature: In 4th-Way terminology this is the main psycho-emotional trait around which one's psychology and false personality are constructed. In this book it is also known as **Blind Spot** because it remains invisible to all but the most sincere and discerning practitioner of self remembering/self observation.

Conscience: the organic link in the **Human Biological Instrument** to the mind and heart of the Creator; the source of real will. It is the will of God in the human body, perhaps (see also: **Will**). Also called by some "Holy Spirit" and by others "Guardian Angel."

Conscious Suffering: in 4th-Way terminology, there are two kinds of human suffering: mechanical (or unconscious) and conscious (or what Mister Gurdjieff called "intentional") suffering.

Consciousness: the elemental life force or intelligence in all sentient beings; the "I Am" sense of Being or Presence; the sense that I exist; free attention without the interference of ego. In humans, it is possible through conscious effort to develop and mature this force to the level of the Creator. Self observation is one means of doing this. The field in which all phenomena, in all worlds, arise.

Contamination: identification, with the body and its functions and conditioning, or with external objects and people; the Blind Spot (see also: **Blind Spot**); the programs placed into the body's energy centers by those well-meaning (or otherwise) but ignorant beings who influenced us in childhood. These programs define, limit and circumscribe the self, life, and the world. They control how and what we see and feel.

Creator: Who knows? Not me. Possibly non-judgmental love; possibly present, here-now; possibly consciousness; possibly conscience.

Ego: the entire psycho-emotional structure, housed not only in the intellectual-emotional-complex, but also in moving center as various postures and movements. It is a collection of memories organized around a central organizing principle, which is **Chief Feature** or **Blind Spot.**

Guru: Guru is not a person. It is a position in the Work, a universal function, and a state or level of consciousness; as such, this function or state has been animated by many humans throughout history. Not all are at the same level of **Consciousness.** It is a state which is ever-growing and changing. Just as any other state of consciousness, there is no top end. This state is characterized, in its most mature phases, by the complete absence of ego or false personality. In its mature phases this state is known as God consciousness, objective consciousness, and impersonal consciousness. At this point, guru is pure non-judgmental love and is transparent to our Creator—guru becomes a transparent channel for our Creator to manifest in the human world. Thus, in this book, the terms guru/God/love are often used interchangeably.

Honest Body: a consciously relaxed body, especially in moments of stress; a body without the unnecessary tensions of identification.

Human Biological Instrument: the human body viewed from a more objective viewpoint. Note that here it is called "instrument" rather than "machine," implying a tool by which one may make minute and careful changes or measurements, and also a tool by which one may make beautiful music.

I Am: In Biblical terms, this is one of the names assigned to our Creator. In spiritual work, this is the designation for the Being whose temporary home is the human body; it is the statement-of-Being, without the addition of **Ego.**

Identification: I am that; the belief that I am only the body or the body's processes or functions, or anything other than Attention.

Intention: from the intellectual center, although it can be deeper, possibly from the Being. When it is combined with wish from emotional center, it can be the beginning of will (see also: **Center, Wish, Will**).

Look from Above: Madame de Salzmann uses this term in her book *The Reality of Being* to indicate a moment of inner stillness and union when one is "seen" by forces above humanity in scale. One is both observing oneself, and is observed from Above.

Mechanical: driven by habit; automatic pilot; unconscious; unaware.

Negative Emotion: all fear-based emotions other than those related to present danger to the organism; those emotions which are not love.

Non-Judgmental Love: As the name implies, this is a love which does not judge. It is the most mature form of love which the soul may manifest. It does not condemn, criticize, or complain. It is characterized by kindness, generosity, forgiveness, apology, and compassion. It is our Creator manifesting in the human world through a clear and transparent channel, a human being who does not interfere with the descending Divine love current which animates all life forms. It is the language of our Creator and the means by which It communicates with Its creation.

Objective: the view of an object or process without the interference of ego, with its beliefs, opinions, judgments, likes and dislikes; that is: without identification with the object or process (see also: **Identification, Ego**)

Practice of Presence: This is the name given in this book to the practice of self remembering/self observation; it indicates the struggle of the sincere practitioner to find and remain present to life, both inner and outer.

Purification of the Centers: what are called "chakras" in some traditions—those points in the body which move and use incoming energy—are called in other traditions "centers;" the main centers discussed in this book are intellectual, emotional, and moving centers. These centers become "contaminated" (programmed and habitually negative) by life experiences. The process of awakening includes, of necessity, the cleansing of contamination of these centers, or chakras. This purification occurs lawfully from the continued sincere Practice of Presence.

Ray of Creation: In the 4th-Way teaching, all worlds are the result of a "ray of creation" emanating from our Creator. Thus, the descending Divine love current, which is our Creator's manifestation in these worlds and which animates and sustains all worlds, descends as this ray of creation and penetrates into every created world.

Sensation: the movement of energy in the body, as revealed by Attention, as well as the input of the five senses, thought, emotion, and impulse.

Soul: (see **Being**).

Voluntary Suffering: different from the ordinary suffering of humanity, which is due to the action of habit and belief systems, expectations and desire; the result of the conscious intention to observe myself honestly, without judgment or trying to change what is observed. Unlike ordinary mechanical suffering, voluntary suffering has the power to transform the Being. Here it is most often called Intentional Suffering, as Mister Gurdjieff indicated.

Will of Attention: the fundamental, minimal ability to consciously direct the attention onto an object or inner process, even in the grip of identification, and when no other action is possible; the ability to see myself as I am in the midst of my daily life.

Will: the conscious focus of intellectual, emotional, and instinctive-moving centers simultaneously upon an object, action, direction, or process; the ability to direct the Attention (see also: **Wish, Aim**).

Wish: The conscious recognition of one's "lack," based on honest self observation and its attendant intentional suffering, gives rise to a wish from the feelings for something to change. Wish can give rise to aim.

Work Circle (or **Inner Work Circle**): the inner, non-judgmental space created by non-identification with what is observed, which allows what arises within me to do so without interference; those small inner "i's" and groups of "i's" which have bonded together to support inner work; the connection of mind and body via sensation, which allows the harmonious working of centers

Work Octave: In 4th-Way terminology, "octave" refers to movement of energy in a system; it also refers to the octaves in the Western musical scale; finally, it refers to the "Law of Seven" as it is represented in the Enneagram. Whenever one undertakes a new direction or task, one begins a new octave. This applies to the inner world as well, where "Practical Work On Self" creates many new Work octaves based on one's self observation and its accompanying shocks.

Work (also **Practical Work on Self**): conscious, intentional inner labor and intentional suffering to remember myself, even in the most trying of circumstances, and to observe myself as I am, without judgment or trying to change what is observed; remembering myself in the midst of my daily life; voluntary suffering as a result of observing myself as I am, without buffers, lying, blaming, or justifying. The Practice of Presence.

References

Almaas, A.H. *Diamond Heart: Book Four.* Boston: Shambhala, 2001.

Brooke, Paul. *Into the Silent Land: Travels in Neuropsychology.* New York: Grove Press, 2003.

Castaneda, Carlos. *The Second Ring of Power.* New York: Simon and Schuster, 1977.

Cleary, Thomas, translator. *Living and Dying with Grace: Counsels of Hadrat Ali.* Boston: Shambhala, 1995.

Collin, Rodney. *The Theory of Celestial Influence.* London: Mercury Publications. 2006.

Conge, Michel. *Inner Octaves.* Toronto: Dolmen Meadow Editions, 2004.

Da Free John. "Killing the Tiger," *Laughing Man* 7:2. 17.

Da Free John. *The Bodily Location of Happiness.* Clearlake, Calif.: The Dawn Horse Press, 1982

de Salzmann, Jeanne. *The Reality of Being: The Fourth Way of Gurdjieff.* Boston: Shambhala, 2010.

Golas, Thaddeus. *The Lazy Man's Guide to Enlightenment.* New York: Bantam Books, 1980.

Gold, E.J. *Life in the Labyrinth.* Nevada City, Calif.: IDHHB, Inc., 1986.

Gold, E.J. *The Joy of Sacrifice: Secrets of the Sufi Way.* Nevada City, Calif.: IDHBB, Inc. and Hohm Press, 1978.

Greenwald, Nachama. *Tawagoto.* 24:1 [Summer/Fall 2011. 82).

Griscom, Chris. *The Healing of Emotion: Awakening the Fearless Self.* New York: Simon & Schuster, 1988.

Gurdjieff, George. *Beelzebub's Tales to His Grandson.* "The Holy Planet Purgatory." New York: Viking Arkana, 1992.

Gurdjieff, George. *Life Is Real Only Then, When "I Am".* New York: E.P. Dutton, 1981.

Gurdjieff, George. *Views From the Real World: Early Talks of Gurdjieff.* New York: E.P. Dutton, 1975.

Kabat-Zinn, Jon. *Coming To Our Senses,* New York: Hyperion Press. 2005.

Lannes, Henriette. *Inside a Question.* London: Paul H. Crompton, 2002.

Lao Tsu. *Tao Te Ching.* Tr. Gia-Fu Feng. New York: Vintage Books, 1972.

Lozowick, Lee. *Chasing Your Tail: Notes That May Be Difficult to Follow On Subjects That May Be Difficult To Grasp.* Prescott, Arizona: Hohm Press, 2009.

Lozowick, Lee. *Intimate Secrets of a True Heart Son.* Chino Valley, Arizona: Hohm Press, 2012.

Lozowick, Lee. *Words of Fire & Faith: A View from the Edge.* "The Will of God." Chino Valley, Arizona: Hohm Press, 2013

Lozowick, Lee. *Tawagoto* 24:1 [Summer/Fall 2011]. 6-7.

Nicoll, Maurice. *Psychological Commentaries.* London: Robinson & Watkins Books, Ltd., 1973.

Osho Rajneesh. *Take It Easy,* vol. 1. Poona, India: Rajneesh Foundation, Ltd., 1979.

Osho Rajneesh. *The Secret of Secrets.* Antelope, Ore: Rajneesh Foundation International, 1982.

Osho. *The Dhammapada, the Way of the Buddha,* Series 11. Portland, Ore.: Rebel Publishing House, n.d.

Ouspensky, Madame. *Talks By Madame Ouspensky.* Manchester, U.K.: Philogos Press, 1974.

Ouspensky, P.D. *In Search of the Miraculous.* New York: Harcourt, Brace & Co., 1949.

Patterson, William Patrick. *Spiritual Survival.* Fairfax, Calif.: Arete Communications, 2009.

Ramana Maharshi. *The Spiritual Teaching of Ramana Maharshi.* Boston: Shambhala, 1988.

Red Hawk. *The Art of Dying.* Prescott, Arizona: Hohm Press, 1999.

Shri Purohit Swami, translator. *The Bhagavad Gita*. New York: Vintage Books, 1977.

Sri Anirvan. "The Awakened Body," *Material for Thought*: 14. 1995.

Tracol, Henri. *The Taste for Things That Are True*. Rockport, Mass.: Element, 1994.

Trungpa, Chögyam Rinpoche. *Crazy Wisdom*. Boston: Shambhala, 2001.

Trungpa, Chögyam Rinpoche. *Shambhala: The Sacred Path of the Warrior*. Boston: Shambhala, 1988.

About the Author

RED HAWK was the Hodder Fellow at Princeton University and currently teaches at the University of Arkansas at Monticello.

Red Hawk may be contacted at **moorer@uamont.edu**

About Hohm Press

HOHM PRESS is committed to publishing books that provide readers with alternatives to the materialistic values of the current culture, and promote self-awareness, the recognition of interdependence, and compassion. Our subject areas include parenting, transpersonal psychology, religious studies, women's studies, the arts and poetry.

Contact Information

Hohm Press, PO Box 4410, Chino Valley, Arizona, 86323; USA; 800-381-2700, or 928-636-3331; email: hppublisher@cableone.net

Visit our website at www.hohmpress.com